Technology With Curves

JoAnn Napier | Denise Shortt | Emma Smith

Technology
With Curves

*Women Reshaping
the Digital Landscape*

📖 HarperCollins*PublishersLtd*

Technology With Curves:
Women Reshaping the Digital Landscape
Copyright © 2000 by JoAnn Napier,
Denise Shortt, Emma Smith.

Technology With Curves is a trademark
of the Wired Woman Society.

www.harpercanada.com

HarperCollins books may be purchased for
educational, business, or sales promotional
use. For information please write:
Special Markets Department,
HarperCollins Canada,
55 Avenue Road, Suite 2900,
Toronto, Ontario, Canada M5R 3L2

First HarperCollins hardcover ed.
ISBN 0-00-200048-2
First HarperCollins trade paper ed.
ISBN 0-00-638634-2

Editor's Note: The profile of Gerry
Laybourne, written by JoAnn Napier,
is part of the Digital Architects' Series.

Canadian Cataloguing in Publication Data

Napier, JoAnn
Technology with curves :
women reshaping the digital landscape

Includes index.
ISBN 0-00-200048-2

I. Women in Technology.
I. Shortt, Denise.
II. Smith, Emma, 1970–   .
III. Title

T36.N36 2000   338.4'762'0082
C00-931226-9

00 01 02 03 04 HC 5 4 3 2 1

Printed and bound in the United States
Set in Monotype Joanna and Univers

TOC

To our mothers
Agnes, Sharon, and Christine

Contents

life

work

culture

introduction 179

Preface

Anyone who doesn't believe in fate doesn't know the story of JoAnn Napier, Denise Shortt, and Emma Smith—the three women who came together to write *Technology With Curves*.

In 1996, years before they would actually all meet, the trio were already connected in several ways.

First, JoAnn, Denise, and Emma all recognized that women's contributions to technology were still often going unacknowledged. Even as more and more women were becoming active in technology fields and making important contributions to the reshaping of the digital landscape, technology careers continued to be viewed as a male domain. Instead, these three women wanted to showcase the unique, non-linear perspectives that women were bringing to technology.

Second, the three women connected through an innovative non-profit organization and Web site.

JoAnn, a technology journalist, had interviewed the Net's male pioneers for two documentaries about the Internet. Now she wanted to explore women's contributions to the digital world, and started researching female pioneers in the field of technology. One day, a friend asked her if she'd contribute an essay to the premier issue of an ezine being launched by the Wired Woman Society, an organization that encouraged women to take hold of the digital reins. JoAnn agreed.

Meanwhile, Denise was at Harvard University, where she co-chaired WIT (Women in Technology), an organization that shared the Wired Woman Society's goal of engaging and empowering women in technology. Denise was also researching gender and computer culture and one night came across the same society Web site. She sent an email to Emma Smith in Vancouver and the two women kicked off a virtual friendship.

Emma had founded the Wired Woman Society in the summer of 1996 in reaction to her experiences working and teaching in the burgeoning world of New Media. As an instructor, she realized that women were under-represented in her classes, and as the cofounder of one of Canada's first Internet communications companies, she saw that same under-representation in business.

Emma and Denise talked about bringing Wired Woman to Toronto, and Denise agreed to take on the task upon returning from Boston.

Jump forward a year or so to the launch of Wired Woman Toronto. Denise and her team of volunteers had lined up high profile guest speakers, negotiated corporate sponsorships, furiously promoted the Toronto launch in the media, and had arranged for Emma to fly in from Vancouver to cut the proverbial ribbon. JoAnn, coincidentally, was there as well. Now a Toronto-based technology columnist, she decided to cover the Toronto Wired Woman launch.

After the standing room only event, JoAnn introduced herself to Denise and they chatted about Denise's experiences studying with cyberspace sociologist Sherry Turkle and JoAnn's interview, just three weeks earlier, with Silicon Valley superstar, Dr. Anita Borg. The women swapped stories about other technology educators, innovators, and leaders and shared their hope that more women in the mainstream could see that the digital landscape was being influenced by these women in unique, impressive ways.

Meanwhile, back in Vancouver, Emma had started interviewing video game designers and Web developers, gathering their stories and taking them out to high schools and speaking engagements to start spreading the word about how women were reshaping the world of technology.

So, finally, it was passion and common purpose that connected these three women. All were in search of stories about women and technology, and each was passionate about finding ways to share those stories. It was now 1999 and, as a massive mainstream infusion of women online began to popularize stories of women and technology, Denise introduced Emma to JoAnn virtually and the three women decided to team up and write *Technology With Curves*.

In June 1999 the women finally had a chance to meet in person. Canada was staging its first Women in New Media Awards and Denise and JoAnn, who'd been asked to be an awards judge, attended the ceremony. When the Outstanding Volunteer Award was announced, it was Emma who accepted. After the ceremony the three women, for the first time, sat down together and talked about projects past, present, and future.

As three talented and diverse authors, JoAnn, Denise, and Emma have come together to explore how women are reshaping the technological landscape. *Technology With Curves* recognizes the contributions of the Digital Dozen, 12 female IT pioneers, and celebrates the stories of many other women around the world who, we hope, will inspire you to explore opportunities of your own.

Welcome to *Technology With Curves*.

Foreword

Achieving the Promise

It took more than 100 years to install the world's first 700 million telephone lines. Yet within the next 10 to 15 years alone, another 700 million lines will be installed and another 700 million people will become mobile phone users as well. All these new connections are having a profound impact on our everyday lives. We needn't line up in banks anymore. We can shop by phone and screen. We can access centuries of learning with the touch of a mouse. And wherever we are on earth, we can be in touch with other people.

The way we do business is also changing—fundamentally. Markets are now global. Customers are truly in control. Smart companies are tearing down old bureaucratic hierarchies and creating flexible, team-oriented learning organizations. More and more, companies are not only competing but also co-operating with each other through partnerships and alliances. Big companies are increasingly outsourcing functions to free agents or creating spin-off companies to capture new markets.

All of this means that new opportunities abound—from setting up your own business to pursuing a career in new fields, such as computer animation, Web site development, and network engineering. Gathered in this book are stories from some of the women who have seen these new opportunities and jumped in, headfirst. Their stories are original and inspiring, and they illustrate the many gifts that women bring to our increasingly wired world.

There are five gifts in particular that I believe women contribute to the world of technology, all of which you will see embodied in the women you'll read about here. And all of which you'll see in the women you meet who are working in today's technology companies, organizations, and start-ups.

Our first gift is *courage*, a quality that is certainly evident in the tremendous entrepreneurial drive being exhibited by women today. You have to be brave, persistent, and take risks to become a successful entrepreneur, even in a world where you can set up a business anytime, anywhere.

Our second gift is *creativity*. Creative and successful businesspeople recognize a customer desire or need, and devise imaginative ways to fulfill it. Many of the women you'll hear about in *Technology With Curves* will showcase the important part creativity plays in technology careers, and the wonderful ways women are bringing this creativity to the environments, software products, and Web sites they're designing.

Our third gift is that of *customer understanding*. Successful entrepreneurs and businesspeople today provide exquisite customer care by constantly listening to and responding to their customers' needs. The reward is profound customer loyalty, which is especially important to high-tech companies who have new competitors springing up every day.

Our fourth gift is *our natural tendency to collaborate*. We're comfortable working in groups. We like to seek out the ideas and perspectives of others. We like to talk things through, and we're good listeners. The true value of any organization lies in its knowledge capital—the information, ideas, and intelligence gained and shared by employees with each other, their partners, and the outside world. And so today's smart technology companies are tapping into their knowledge capital by building learning organizations where collaboration fuels growth and innovation.

Which brings me to the fifth gift that I believe women are bringing to high-tech. This gift is passion—a passion for change and a profound caring about the future. Many women have a deep desire to make the world a better place and are hoping to play a role in ensuring that technology is implemented wisely and responsibly.

Many of the female scientists and leaders I work with at Lucent Technologies Canada Inc., and many of the women you'll read about in *Technology With Curves*, demonstrate such a passion. The wired world is the perfect stomping ground for passionate change agents, as we see each time a motivated person carves out a new path or founds a start-up.

Emma Smith, founder of the Wired Woman Society, is one of these women.

One fateful afternoon in 1996, Emma and five of her friends met at a Vancouver café. They chatted, caught up on the news, and vented their frustrations about working in male-dominated, money-hungry technology firms that often seemed to overlook human interaction. Soon the conversation turned to the need for an organization that would support women getting into IT (Information Technology). That night, Emma decided to make the Wired Woman Society a reality.

Today, the Wired Woman Society has almost 1000 members. It is now a national organization dedicated to creating an open environment that can help women explore opportunities in technology. Wired Woman's 100 volunteers are change agents in their own right, who now work hard to offer technology education camps, mentoring programs, extensive networking opportunities, and monthly professional development sessions in the society's chapters across the country. Wired Woman also supports special initiatives to encourage young girls to pursue careers in IT, and acts as a powerful voice for Canadian women interested in technology.

It was Emma's passion for change that led her to create Wired Woman, and it is also through Wired Woman that Emma met fellow change agents Denise Shortt and JoAnn Napier. Together these three women have collected the stories they believe illustrate the wonderful gifts women are bringing to the Wired World.

These authors, like so many in the field, are committed to doing their part to ensure that women make a full and meaningful contribution to shaping technology. Women are passionate about sharing ideas and skills, and having an impact on the wider sphere of events. These assets, along with the gifts of courage, creativity, customer understanding, collaboration, and passion are of incredible value to the workplace and the marketplace. Use your gifts well—for your sake, for your company's sake, for the world's sake. And enjoy these stories from women who are out there putting their gifts into action.

Carol M. Stephenson
President and CEO
Lucent Technologies Canada Inc.

life

introduction

How do we harness the power of technology to improve our lives? The women in this section of this book will answer that question. They are digital architects. Some are powerful people whose professional insights, networks of influence, and unique alliances set them apart. Others lead more ordinary lives. They are mothers, sisters, daughters, wives—all are bridging gaps that impact the way we live.

Some are closing gaps between research and commerce, to ensure that the pillars of our wired world are rooted in public interest. Others are closing gaps in access to technology, and gender gaps in the design of high-tech products by developing tools for living that extend, and improve, our lives. All are bridging gaps in the public consciousness, by sparking an appreciation of women as inventors and influencers of technology.

No two lives are the same, and men's and women's lives are defined differently—by society and economics, culture and biology. Differences exist, too, in the balance of power in our world. And the Internet is our first vital, virtual tool for living: it can shift the power by letting the user take charge. Interactive technology is not passive. Every minute of every day, anyone with online access can speak up and be heard. A virtual voice can echo, and influence.

This reality was revealed to me one summer evening in the early 1990s while working on a documentary about the Internet's founding fathers. A simple Net connection and email account let me both research, and reach, the seminal thinkers and key players of the Internet: Tim Berners-Lee, Mark Andreessen, Vinton Cerf, Paul Baran, Marc Weiser all heard my virtual call, and answered.

That night, a final email arrived just before midnight. It

began: "I didn't know who else to email, and I hope you don't mind but I just found a lump in my breast." A 43-year-old housewife, on the other side of the continent, had slipped out of bed and while her husband and toddlers slept, crept downstairs to type out those words. She was using a family computer to home-school her children and we'd exchanged email messages about collaborating on a TV documentary segment. We'd never met. But in that moment, this woman—this mother, wife, and daughter—revealed the real power of technology: one person, gripped by cold fear, reached out and initiated a profoundly powerful exchange.

Technology is a tool. It can improve the way we live if we wield it well. Consumers hold the power in the digital revolution, and women—who tend to measure technology's value by its usefulness—also, traditionally, hold the domestic purse-strings. Technology is about to assume a very practical, more ubiquitous, role as a tool in our homes and workplaces. In our everyday lives. How will digital life now be altered by women? Read on.

JoAnn Napier

Zoë Baird
"Weaving Public Good into the Net"

www.markle.org

What if you were given hundreds of millions of dollars, and a mission: To improve people's lives? Welcome to Zoë Baird's world. As head of the New York–based Markle Foundation, Baird has the opportunity and the resources to make a difference. The philanthropic foundation's war chest—more than $100 million (US)—is being funneled into Net-related projects. Interactive media cannot be used passively, says Baird, and the Internet, and Internet industry, must be made to work for the public good. But timing is everything; the pillars of our high-speed, new-millennium landscape are being cast. Which is why Baird is moving fast, working hard, and spending big.

Zoë Baird is carrying a lot on her shoulders. As president of

the Markle Foundation, this accomplished American attorney and corporate executive has been given an extraordinary opportunity. Two opportunities, really: the chance to figure out how to improve life in the Information Age, and access to the kind of cash that can make a difference.

Zoë buckled down to this monumental task by launching a

comprehensive review of the communications landscape. She and her Markle colleagues heard experts' opinions and considered research drawn from a spectrum of professions and industrial influences. What surfaced were some simple truths. Zoë discovered she had assumed the helm of this philanthropic organization at an historic moment in time: the Wild West period in the communications arena was ending. New, long-term commercial, cultural, social, and institutional pillars were beginning to be established. So, decisions made today would have a lasting impact.

Big opportunities are often wed to big risks, and even bigger dilemmas. She wrestled with weighty concerns— "How does one pave the way for progress while reinforcing our values and institutions? How do you harness the potential of new media to improve people's lives?"—and she rooted many decisions in this simple, yet profound, credo: Interactive media cannot be used passively. Internet business, Zoë believes, must be focused on the big picture. And that scenario requires the Internet to work for the public good. The Internet industry is awash in capital, and Markle has the money "to act as a bridge between research and commerce— and turn public interest into marketplace realities."

The foundation's intensive study of the new media landscape exposed four areas of specific need: public engagement, children, health care, and communications policy. And it underscored the need to focus on one key issue: access. Despite the rate at which technology is coming into many lives, the so-called digital divide—the gap in access to technology, and specifically computers and the Internet (see sidebar, p. 13)—has been growing in the United States in recent years. Zoë says the explosive growth in this field has not occurred evenly across boundaries of race, education, and income—and that reality underscores the very real possibility that some people will be left out of the new digital society entirely.

"As I said at the [1999 conference on the Digital Divide] at the White House, access alone is not enough. People in low-income communities will soon be able to access the Internet through cellular phones and other ways. We really need to focus on content and services, on how this technology can improve their lives, and we believe that interactive media has a tremendous potential to do just that . . . if we consciously attend to making that happen."

In the summer of 1999, Zoë announced that the Markle Foundation would spend $100 million (US)—half of its war chest—on various Internet ventures in the next three to five years. In an interview in March 2000, Zoë said she believes the next three to five years are the critical period for influencing policy and "architecting" a digital industry infrastructure that reflects public interest. The largest of the initial awards went to Oxygen Media, headed by another of our Digital Dozen profiled in this book: **Geraldine Laybourne** (see p. 79).

Other U.S. foundations are funding some Internet projects—for example, the Ford, Rockefeller, and MacArthur foundations; Markle is neither the only foundation, nor the largest, in the mix. But the foundation Zoë heads has historically been recognized for setting precedents and strategic policy paths that other philanthropic organizations have followed. And it's been praised for making the first move in trying to push the Net in the direction of serving the public good.

Under Zoë's direction, Markle is spending money about 10 times faster than it normally does—seriously siphoning off funds that tallied about $180 million (US) at the time of the 1999 announcement. The foundation is now devoted entirely to funding Net projects. That's just how important the medium is, she says.

This dramatic move to invest in reshaping the digital landscape for the public good is an updated reflection of Markle's original mandate. Formed in 1927 with money from a Pennsylvania coal family, the foundation—in more recent times—has funded many mass-media projects and specialized in grants that link communications with public needs. Markle was one of the key early supporters of American public television. There are lessons to be learned from history and she intends to learn from the mistakes of the past. In the 1950s, she says, foundations missed the opportunity to participate in shaping the business models for television. By the time foundations became heavy donors to educational public television and radio in the late 1960s, it was too late: the commercially sustainable models for this new communications medium had already been established, and public-television programming was not a built-in priority.

Zoë notes this is not the first time new media has promised to improve the way we live. "In radio's early years, the medium was seen to have characteristics analogous to those of the Internet today. There was great expectation that radio would transform democracy, create communities across borders, and produce a more educated and enlightened population. Amateur use dominated radio in the early 1900s; before 1928, more than 95 percent of radio broadcasters were noncommercial. Soon, however, commercial broadcasters began to dominate the airwaves, and although radio has done much for society, it never fulfilled its potential as an informational or community-building tool."

Television's story is similar. From the late 1940s to the early 1950s, the medium was the focus of extensive experimentation and innovation by the broadcast networks. Once they identified profitable business models, however, these models predominated for decades. "The moment of opportunity to build societal needs into the business of the television industry was lost," she says. By the time public television was formed almost two decades later, it was essentially "tacked on" to a commercial system that had already been established. "Other public needs were met periodically as regulatory requirements came and went, and as dedicated people in the industry, and outside it, worked to influence its practices. But it has not been possible for television to achieve its potential by trying to retrofit it with social objectives."

Now Markle is giving money to such well-supported enterprises as Oxygen. Why? Because it's the big Internet firms that can reach the masses. "If I wanted to go out and encourage people to read books, what's the best way to do it? [Oxygen partner] Oprah Winfrey can go on TV and bring books to a huge number of women, who in turn set an example for their children. I've seen the trailer of Oprah's program showing women how to use the Internet, and it's pretty impressive," Zoë told reporters when she announced the Oxygen award. "We're setting some goals for Oxygen that they just couldn't justify for themselves." The lion's share of that $4.5-million award was earmarked to create a separate business: Oxygen–Markle Pulse, an initiative designed to gather audience feedback from Oxygen's Web and cable properties and distribute that information to the public in a bid to make sure new media content reflects the public voice.

It's clear to Zoë, a mother of two young boys, that information technology is going to transform the world her sons live in—transform their values and the way people relate to each other. Some Markle initiatives fall outside its primary program areas; for example, the foundation assisted the International Rescue Committee in developing and implementing the software-based Child Connect program to reunite refugees with their families, and the Kosovar Family Finder, a database-driven project that provides refugees with the location information of displaced family and friends. But Markle is focusing on developing areas ranging from children's media to health, and on policy decisions affecting these new media.

Regardless of the area, all Markle projects are essentially oriented toward one question, she says: What kind of world should our children be living in? For example, Markle is developing a national research agenda to gain in-depth knowledge about the impact of interactive media on the cognitive, emotional, physical, and development needs of children, and focuses on integrating this knowledge into the creation of children's products and services. ("Some studies are beginning to show that boys playing a lot of games on computers is not, in fact, an isolating experience but, rather, gives kids who aren't into sports—or don't have other obvious ways of talking to other kids—ways to relate to other children . . . We need to know more, because we need to know whether this is really good for kids or not.")

Certainly, today's children grow up in a culture saturated by television, handheld video games, computer games. Interactive games and toys compete for kids' time and attention. Many children, Zoë notes, are on the Net before they enter school. Like other parents, she wonders about the fallout: Which interactive experiences are valuable for children? Which ones will help them build skills? Which ones should be avoided, in what way, and at what ages? The foundation, through initiatives such as a $2-million (US) ad campaign, is helping parents to understand the potential of interactive media for their children.

"One of the things that I was interested in was the research that shows children learn best from interacting with the world around them, and that they are very much aided in their learning by positive reinforcement. Those things are not new . . . but when you put that together with a computer, I see my four-year-old excitedly saying, 'Mom, Mom! I just moved to the next level!' And it's thrilling for him to have achieved something concrete in the world around him. It's another kind of achievement . . .

and it's hard to think how you replicate that. A protective environment where he can have success on his own," she says. "And then kids that don't have a mom who's making a choice about whether or not to be there, but rather a mom who can't be there much. Can that child have that same experience? [During] those hours that they're spending at home, being babysat by a big brother or aunt or being in a foster home, can they have that same experience? And can we help that experience? You know, computers are no substitute for human contact. Interactive media experience is no substitute for a good education. But, boy, it can help."

Another area of vital interest to Zoë and her foundation is Internet governance. The first initiative of Markle's Internet Governance Project was to commit more than $1 million to activities intended to promote the public interest in avenues where nations are ceding authority to make decisions, and standards, governing activities on the Internet. Close to half of that funding is expected to go to a set of initiatives aimed at ICANN, the Internet's first oversight body, which is chaired by another of our Digital Dozen, Esther Dyson (see p. 67). Why fund ICANN? Zoë says that, in being handed the responsibility by the United States government for managing the Internet's core domain name system worldwide, ICANN is officially wrestling with so-called technical issues. But, in reality, ICANN is wrestling with a host of related problems that can, ultimately, impact critical issues of free speech, free competition, and representation.

She wants to make sure ICANN has the resources and range of voice needed to answer questions such as "How do we make sure this new policymaking is responsive to public needs?" ICANN, for example, must determine how to balance anonymity on the Web—a key element of political freedom—with the right to know who's behind a domain name. Zoë points to the case of B92, the courageous independent radio station in Belgrade that had its online identity (b92.net) taken over and used by Slobodan Milosevic, and was left with no avenue for recourse.

Should ICANN have acted? "In many instances," Zoë says, "the decision whether or not to act will have main policy implications." As our digital landscape grows globally, there is no "established playbook" to work from; decisions are being made which will have widespread implications for the public, and they will only be legitimate if the public is involved in how they are made, she says. "This is not some bloodless debate," Zoë told the ICANN board at their annual meeting in November 1999. "We have all read stories about the Web site listing of doctors performing abortions and crossing them off as they were targets for assassination. Or the Web site that published alleged British intelligence agents and put lives and, potentially, British national security at risk. We have a hard time seeing the validity of the claim to anonymity (online). . . . but in the case of Chinese dissidents, we may have a different view."

Asked who are the people who most influence the way she does her job, Zoë points to her two young boys. "I probably wouldn't be doing this if I didn't have young children. It's so clear to me that information technology is going to transform the world they live in, transform their values and the way people relate to each other—the way business is done, the job opportunities, and the opportunities for personal satisfaction that they feel. It's going to transform the place of our nation in the world, as this medium becomes global. And that belief is very much the reason why I am, at every opportunity, trying to promote or trying to achieve the greatest potential for society from this medium—rather than allowing it to become whatever it might be. It's why I care so deeply about [digital technology's] influence."

To ensure the public voice echoes resoundingly on the Net; to help us grow up and grow old with technology that reflects our core values. This is Zoë Baird's mission in the new millennium.

The Digital Divide

The so-called digital divide—the growing gap between the haves and have-nots of the information age—is growing wider: people, entire countries in fact, are being left behind as technology races ahead. Who's falling through the Net, specifically? Racial minorities, the poor, people in rural areas and developing countries.

Social and economic gaps contributing to our digital divide spell serious economic consequences. Jobs in the fastest-growing markets all depend on having high-technology skills. Understanding the language of the Net and being able to use its material is part of a new, basic survival literacy.

In the U.S. and Canada, millions of dollars in federal funding have started pouring into programs and initiatives aimed at connecting classrooms and citizens. Some support is being directed to community technology centers in poor and isolated areas where home computer ownership is a rarity. Other efforts are focused on advocating policies aimed at deregulating the telecommunications industry, which could make online connections at home more affordable to the poor.

Technology can't just be put out there: training must be part of the package. Recognizing this reality, a coalition of 180 of America's largest civil rights groups have launched an initiative to empower the civil rights community via leadership forums and modern-day "freedom riders" who will bring high-tech training to the doorsteps of nonprofit organizations.

Federal Communications Commission member Michael Powell says the digital revolution is minorities' first big chance to become empowered. Unlike the agricultural revolution or the industrial revolution, users hold the power in the digital revolution. The decentralized nature of the Net gives start-up firms a chance to compete with established companies. Users have the potential to innovate, to develop product, to distribute product—to take charge. Powell believes the minority community needs to focus on becoming part of the producing class, and not just the consuming class.

True empowerment comes from having the means to make bread, not just eating the crumbs left by another baker, Powell believes. The U.S. Commerce Department's National Telecommunications and Information Administration has established a Web site that identifies a range of grant and loan programs that provide assistance to people vulnerable to falling on the Net, and ending up on the wrong side of the digital divide. The site provides direct links to educational and funding resources aimed at closing the divide through private-sector partnerships: initiatives such as *Oprah Goes Online*, a cable TV series focusing on how to use a computer, and America Online's partnership with the Benton Foundation, which provides a clearing house of IT information and resources—a one-stop shop for local communications.

Meanwhile, progress in developing regions is slow. Perhaps nothing better underscores the divide than the realities reflected at the 1999 annual meeting of the Internet Society. While the nonprofit group's representatives from developing countries were discussing how to connect their people to the digital world, 40 percent of all venture capital money invested in the new digital economy was circulating just outside the conference doors—within a 40-mile radius of a Silicon Valley conference center.

Lynn Harris

Online Advice Columnist and Cocreator of Breakup Girl
www.breakupgirl.com

A freelance writer and stand-up comedian, Lynn Harris is partnered with her platonic roommate/artist/friend Chris Kalb; together, they created Breakup Girl, an online dating advice column, complete with essays and a quirky comic strip. Breakupgirl.com drew 45,000 visitors a month shortly after Lynn and Chris posted it online. Now, Breakup Girl is going to have her chance to hit the small screen in her animated series on the Oxygen Media cable network.

Back in 1998, the *New York Times* carried a tiny item saying that Robert Morton, a former producer for David Letterman, had taken a real shine to Breakup Girl. The item noted Morton "wanted to swell Breakup Girl's following to millions by making her a star on a television network, starting with ABC." Lynn says her life changed after that item appeared. Morton's television production company, Panamort, optioned the character for television, and then Geraldine Laybourne's (see p. 79) team at Oxygen Media made an offer of acquisition and employment. "Acquisition of everything," said Lynn. Not just the character, but the site,

Breakup Girl speaks on popularity.

I still have my dork moments, but I generally think I'm pretty cool. Pretty comfortable with myself, pretty happy with my haircut. Fun friends, interesting plans, spiffy clothes, the occasional cute boy, even. If I were in school right now, I might even be popular.

That's now.

Back in seventh grade, things did not look so promising. Especially not through BG's huge thick heinous glasses.

This week, let's focus clearly on the "P" word. Because more often than not, there's no "u" in POPULARITY.

See, I had started at a new school that, at first, might as well have been

and Lynn's and Chris's services to keep producing and developing their original creation. ("Plus an animated series—which is ideal—landed on the table. So, in a friendly turnover [it turns out, coincidentally, that Panamort is Oxygen's TV casting company], Panamort's option was bought out by Oxygen as part of the whole deal.")

How has this development changed Breakup Girl's life, as well as the professional routine of its creators? Lynn says it's allowed Breakup Girl to become bigger, better, and able to serve more people. Lynn and Chris made a decision to ramp up Breakup Girl in two areas: entertainment and especially service. The advice offerings, for instance, were changed to make it clearer to people that different avenues and options existed ("besides waiting, fingers crossed, for their letter to be answered") to get information and feedback. And new sites were conceived, such as vitaminBreakupGirl.com, a special Breakup Girl site for teens on healthy relationships.

Breakup Girl's also getting a chance to hit the small screen in her animated series. And since Lynn is Breakup Girl's alter ego, she'll have her own regular segments on new Oxygen shows such as *Trackers*, an afternoon show that involves roving teenage girls with digital cameras who create episodes that deal with fashion, movies, boys, and getting into college.

How has all this success affected her personally? Lynn says she'd reached the age of 30 without ever owning a car or being a salaried employee. She *still* doesn't have a car. But now, she says, she wears shoes to work. ("Especially because I could be called to be on air at any moment. Also because I am crazy about shoes—but that's a different story.")

Time Digital wrote: "What sets Breakup Girl apart from Dear Abby and Ann Landers? About 50 years and a wicked sense of humor." Lynn believes part of Breakup Girl's appeal is rooted in the fact that neither she nor Chris has an ax to grind in their column. And their column has one clear advantage over Dear Abby and her counterparts—cyberspace. "The [others have] x column inches; I've got endless room to print entertainingly nano-detailed soap operas, to wander into literary digressions, to create circles and series of hyperlinks that make the column the center-piece of a world unto itself. Can't do that in x inches in two dimensions."

As for that producer who got things rolling for Breakup

a foreign country where no one spoke my language or looked like—or at—me. Nerd Girl so did *not* belong. I watched in awe as the Popularinas picked up lacrosse sticks and just knew how to play, like in "Fame," where the music starts and every-one in the cafeteria just knows the song. How did they do that? I remember sitting at my desk creating a chart called "Making Friends," with a "+" column and a "-" column. As in "+: talked to Allison Sweeney for five minutes on lunch line," or "-: no one is wearing ribbon barrettes anymore!!!"

No wonder I felt like a loser.

Lynn Harris

Girl, Robert Morton has been quoted as saying, "For years, movies and novels and other different media influenced television . . . As time has gone on, now it's the Web." Does Lynn think his assessment that the Web is now a significant medium of influence is accurate?

"Hmm. I can't speak with much experience as to how the Web might influence the creation of TV, though of course we've seen it happen. I mean, TV is always looking for stuff to mine for new ideas, and new media is one of them. But I do know that any smart show [or movie] now knows that a real, good, solid, value-added Web presence [*Blair Witch Project*, freaks and geeks, Dawson's Desktop], versus sites that offer surfers a chance to 'Just click here to download pictures of your favorite stars!,' is indispensable for audience numbers and loyalty. And for building the shows to icon/cultural 'me-me' status."

Lynn believes that in this day of "self-help, confessional, designer disorders and general McPsychology," people really prolong and indulge their breakups longer than they need to—doing themselves a disservice in the process. "Over at breakupgirl.com, people, even the heartbroken, can have a jaunty, if rueful, sense of humor about life crisis. And that's what we mean to draw out and showcase, especially through things like our annual haiku contest [**www.breakupgirl.com/vday/haiku.html**]. And I meant that not just as a plug for Breakup Girl, but also as a plug for, like, people. That humans have the capacity to create an empathetic, warmly funny breakup oeuvre that, yes, serves . . . well, maybe not as revenge, but as recasting what happened in your own words. Which is how you—to wax biblical—have dominion over it."

Lynn and Chris invented Breakup Girl, the Web site, while writing and designing the first Breakup Girl book. (A second book, *Breakup Girl to the Rescue*, is due out in 2000.) Lynn was inspired by real life; after she broke up with her

boyfriend, she was miserable. "So miserable that my hilari-
ous best friend and I made up jokes and games that made
me cry until I laughed. I sensed that there was something
there . . . I mean, we thought we needed a superhero for
this sort of thing."

Dorothy Spence
and Linda Weaver
"Telemedicine Women"

www.tecknowledge.com

Dorothy Spence and Linda Weaver helped build what many consider the world's most active telehealth network, and they did it from an isolated perch on the North Atlantic coast. The duo are designing technology that takes medicine to the people, and proving innovation and digital partnerships can develop anywhere.

Even at high noon, it is cold on the bridge spanning Halifax Harbour. Passing over Navy frigates nestled in the shipyard below, a driver spots the figure of a man perched atop a billboard near the tollgate, feet dangling. He is clad in little more than a blue business suit, with a laptop computer balanced on his thighs. Off to the right, a

psychiatric hospital sits on a hill; to the left is a sprawling industrial park filled with incubator malls, warehouses, and doughnut shops. This billboard cowboy could have sprung loose from either bunker; the driver takes a closer look. Below the businessman's feet reads a caption: "From here, he's connected to the world."

Dorothy Spence and Linda Weaver, cofounders of TecKnowledge Healthcare Systems Inc., could be sitting up there instead: the peculiar billboard advertisement was paid for by the local telephone company, which is a major investor in their company. From an isolated corporate perch in an industrial mall on the edge of the North Atlantic, these women are designing high-tech networks and helping health-care professionals broaden their worlds and their ways.

Telemedicine, the use of technology to deliver medical care remotely, is a fresh frontier, and Canada is considered a global leader in the industry. The telehealth network in Nova Scotia, designed by Dorothy and Linda—both engineers with MBAs—is considered by many to be the most active telehealth network in the world; it connects dozens of hospitals and uses a hybrid of technologies, from computers, telecommunications and video conferencing equipment to electronic medical instruments. Blood and guts used to be the business of medicine; now, it's bits and bytes as data, X-rays, and expert feedback are being digitized and shared in real time. Technology is taking geography out of the equation.

Generally speaking, telemedicine systems today often use a sophisticated version of a telephone to transmit audio and still images between a remote site and a full-care hospital. This phone is a combination of a handset and video camera at an isolated community, plus a monitor at the hospital. Often used to transmit data, text, still images, and limited-motion video, the Internet is a great health-care tool but, because of the amount of data that needs to be transmitted in order to provide an accurate and reliable diagnosis, it's considered still too slow and unwieldy for most telemedicine applications. Instead, videoconferencing systems with built-in microphones, cameras, scanners, microscopes, stethoscopes, and other medical instruments are often used to transmit data over dedicated phone lines. A Codec machine compresses and decompresses video signals, making transmission faster and providing near broadcast-quality video of patients in remote rural areas or prisons.

Video, diagnostic, and telecommunications equipment is now linking doctors and patients to specialists miles away who can examine, diagnose, and treat illnesses ranging from hypertension to HIV infection. Advances in communications are bringing health care to our doorsteps today; tomorrow, industry experts agree, anything is possible.

Dorothy, who is president and chief executive officer, and Linda, "head techie" and, officially, chief technical officer, are shaping that future by paving telehealth's technology pathways. While working as consultants in the health-care industry in the early 1990s, they switched their focus to telemedicine—still mostly a research-based field at that time. With their knowledge of engineering, health care, technology, and business, the pair found themselves uniquely qualified to work in the field. They went into partnership because they wanted to have control over their lives. It took personal courage: giving up their secure contracts, moving out of their cramped but economical home-office quarters ("Every time we pushed our chairs back at the same time, we crashed into each other"). But by the turn of the millennium, they'd become acknowledged telehealth network innovators.

Soon they were concentrating on new terrain—telehome care—a new telemedicine trend being driven by health-care providers who hope to cut costs, and by advocates who say the practice actually increases the attention given to patients. Hospital administrators say telehome systems are helping to shorten hospital stays. Doctors find it useful for homebound patients such as the elderly. And as high-capacity Internet lines spread to ordinary households, the practice of telehome care is expected to become more widespread.

TecKnowledge's latest telehome project is progressing thanks to funding from a private–public-sector partnership that reflects the niches linked by telemedicine: the project's partners are the hospital, the federal health department, the local telephone company, and a community access center. At Toronto's Hospital For Sick Children, Dorothy and Linda's company collaborated on designing an integrated service that allows a transfer of knowledge between the very specialized tertiary-care nurse in the hospital's Intensive Care Unit to the home-care nurse. Translation: their work will allow children who are patients at the hospital, and who require their vital signs to be monitored, to go home. "You know, only a small number of nurses have that specialization. How do you make this family comfortable; how do you integrate that service and coordinate it? We are collaborating in designing a fairly sophisticated service that lets these children be monitored on a seven-day-a-week, 24-hour-a-day basis through the Kids' Line at the [hospital]," says Dorothy.

The duo look at what clinical service they want to provide, then create the model. But their designs go beyond the technology. There are the people, the roles, the policies, and procedures to consider. Health care is not a process that you can write down on paper, says Linda. "A lot of health care is about relationships: the doctors who went to school together, the nurses who went to school together. When you create a network, what you're doing is webbing the whole environment, and it's not very linear."

Medicine, she says, is both a science and an art. Building a network that connects professionals who are well educated, smart, and independent is tricky. "You have to work with them. They have to work with you, and every time we design something, it evolves and changes and becomes much more rich because of all the factors that come into play, the people and all of the things that are involved."

Regardless of the project, the premise behind their work is always the same. "The technology has to work for the users: if the person using their system says it doesn't work for them, then it just doesn't work," says Linda. "[We] always take the view that you have to meet the users' requirements as opposed to imposing something upon them." How do you create a system that works effectively, while reflecting the range of needs and perspectives inherent in any health-care solution? "That's typically the biggest challenge," says Linda. As "head techie" she's stretched in one direction; Dorothy, who courts clients and investors, is usually stretched in another direction. "And when we talk about where the middle part is, that's where things tend to work the best."

Dorothy adds: "But I've got to tell you that's very much a female approach." The women recognize that there is another kind of approach or orientation to integrating technology and users. "I don't like to label it 'male' or 'female,'" she says. "But the reality is that it has characteristics that are more—call it 'ying' and 'yang,' or whatever, but we view technology as a support mechanism and as a tool. Which is very much what we call the female approach. A collaborative network. Open. Sharing . . . abundancy. All those words. Whereas an opposite approach—and I am not saying it's male, but an opposite approach—is very much where you impose the box on someone. It's a closed system. The network you create can't call anyone outside of the network."

Their vision for telehealth networks was rooted in that female approach. "We wanted to establish a network [in Nova Scotia] that had the capability of the tentacles just going everywhere," says Dorothy. "So wherever you were in this network, you could communicate with anybody else on this network—as well as with people outside the network who were using non-network standards as their technology base. So . . . we designed this with the assumption that people were going to . . . need to connect and communicate with people not only in their own local environment, but people in their regional environment, provincial environment, and national environment. . . . They can feed information in, and know that they can send anywhere."

Dorothy and Linda pride themselves on designing systems that give health-care professionals options, instead of limits. Options that provide users of their telehealth systems with the capability of looking at other ways of doing things. Options that let them approach problems from a grassroots level, and broaden their approach rather than letting the technology dictate what can be done. What appeals to Linda is the idea of "taking technology and doing something in the health-care environment that can help evolve the whole health-care system." Dorothy is focused on where the duo will take their company. They're developing an expansion plan to move into the U.S. market, and are mulling over how to transform their telehealth company into an e-health company.

Telemedicine's "black eye" of embarrassment is the reality that major sums of money—"millions and hundreds of millions of dollars"—are being used to

Linda Weaver and Anita Borg point out that because the engineering world is dominated by men, today's technology and system designs primarily reflect a male approach and perspective. Systems designed for our world will be strengthened, says Anita, by reflecting the diversity of experience both men and women bring to an equation.

As engineers designing technology, men and women will approach things differently, says Linda. "Engineering is very much a group environment, and men should support women [in engineering]. But without women in the mix, designs won't be strengthened by diversity. Ten people from different backgrounds will approach a problem in 10 different ways; an

deploy technology in North America, which is not getting used because it's not well integrated in a clinical environment.

"We've shown people will use it with the right environment. And that knowledge translates directly into an e-health provision of services," says Dorothy, "where you just pay every time you use a [telehealth] service, every time there is a clinical consultation." She's working on how to make TecKnowledge deliver those digital solutions. "When you make information digital, when you make knowledge digital, that changes the rules."

"What we're doing here is the same thing. We are digitizing knowledge and expertise—and it's going to transform the health-care system. It's going to make it possible for patients to stay at the center of the system and have the resources, the knowledge, and expertise come to them."

As Dorothy speaks, somewhere in suburban Philadelphia a physician is working out of a local mall, virtually: at $15 per visit, he examines patients from afar using digital instruments. Meanwhile, at the South Pole, a woman bunkered in a scientific station discovers a lump in her breast; thanks to digital devices, she is able to receive a level of care very close to what she'd receive in her hometown. And that's 1999.

By 2019—or sooner—you may be packing a bio-chip smart card that includes your genetic code and instantly tests your system's reaction to a particular drug. You may wear wristbands that measure sugar levels through the skin and signal artificial pumps in the pancreas to supply insulin, or memory glasses with built-in microcameras which help you recognize familiar faces even though you suffer from Alzheimer's. A scale in your bathroom may double as a home monitoring machine and feed your vital signs, via a TV-top box, to the local hospital. "Who would have thought 15 years ago you could go up to a brick wall and punch in a bunch of numbers and a machine would give you currency from the country that you were in—and have it automatically debited back to your account in Canada?" says Dorothy.

engineer who's a father with a two-year-old, and an engineering mother with a two-year-old, will come up with very different solutions."

Both Linda and Anita draw hope from the progress made by women in medicine—a profession long dominated by men but in which women now thrive. So how do we get young women more interested in engineering, technology, and hard-research sciences? "We have to help people achieve success by creating networks, by identifying each other, and then sharing publicly what we are doing and showing how people are succeeding," says Linda. "Until we have something for people to point at, they won't see any future in it."

Or that these two women, from the edge of a continent, could create a digital blueprint for a new-millennium approach to the science and art of medicine?

Annie Wood

President
Inventive Women Inc.
www.inventivewomen.com

Imagine a world where you can peel back the layers of time
and space and discover the history of women's creativity.
Forget Benjamin Franklin and Thomas Edison. We're talking
inventors in hoopskirts and high heels. Women, of course,
have been creating for a while now. But female inventors
and innovators of products and new technology are not
well known. Annie Wood is out to change all that.

When she was an art teacher, a student once asked her a
question: "Do women invent?" Annie set about researching
the subject, and ended up creating a workshop for her
class, so that her students could educate themselves about
female inventors and their impact. That workshop led,
down the road, to a Web site and to connections among
women, creativity, and inventions. Today, Annie and her

colleagues at Inventive Women
are creating a ripple in our
collective consciousness, making
us aware of women as agents of
technological change.

You have to be a bit of a
dreamer to really appreciate the
beauty of Annie's ways. She
dreamed up the idea of an
educational and interactive Web
site devoted entirely to female

inventors, and was preparing to launch in fall 2000 when we interviewed her. The site—in its beta testing form—looks like a cyber city. Its library holds women's profiles; there's a shopping center where modern female inventors can test-market their products; at the school, students and teachers can learn about female inventors via online activities; in the movie theater, you can see first-person women's stories—"heritage moments"; and at the business center you can access practical information on how to patent and sell an invention.

Inventive Women is a Web site and a wealth of information, but it's also, potentially, much more: a television documentary, educational videos and teacher kits, and a CD-ROM are all in the works. But first, at its origin, Inventive Women was just a notion in the head of a dark-haired, creative mother of Macedonian roots whose eyes flash with intelligence and something akin to irreverence. Annie says her idea initially took a simpler shape, in the form of a one-hour documentary called *The Pink Lab Coat*. Her project eventually evolved into new-media formats. "I wasn't intimidated about building a Web site. I tend to come up with concepts and approaches and simply assume that it's possible to implement them," says Annie, who brings a solid business and publishing/production background to the venture.

As cofounder of Kids Can Press, one of Canada's leading children's book publishers, Annie (who also penned the award-winning children's book *The Sandwich*) published books that reflected Canadian multiculturalism. Today, Kids Can Press is perhaps most famous as the publisher of the Franklin books, which follow the life and adventures of a young turtle and his friends. "When Kids Can Press started, the Canadian children's publishing industry was just a glimmer in the eye. The founding members of the press, including myself, were enthusiastic publishing neophytes committed to the telling of stories of groups in society that had previously been ignored. All aspects of the Canadian children's publishing industry were in their infancy. The skills that I acquired during my half a dozen years at Kids Can Press are the skills that I use at Inventive Women."

She sees the differences between book publishing and Web publishing as both simple and complex. Web publishing, when done well, increases access to information, ideas, and people in unique ways; the Web has the powerful ability to create communities of people of inter- est; the online medium creates a forum and allows content to be shifted and, in part, created by the end-user. "All this happens very quickly and allows for spin- offs between individuals and groups—an instantaneous outreach tool."

Book publishing has always been able to do this in a smaller way, she says, pointing to examples such as tradi- tional book clubs and, more recently, entertainment/community center bookstores such as Chap- ters. But book publishing primarily creates products that are used privately, says Annie, and herein lies the challenge: "With both mediums, content is at the heart. A good story makes for a good read in book publishing. Creating content for the Web is a lot more difficult. Few sites have the abil- ity to excite, inform, inspire, touch the senses, and advance people's lives."

A few years back, Annie decided to produce an exhibition celebrating her roots. Research for the show, entitled "From Baba's Hope Chest: Macedonian Treasure in Canada," required her to visit to more than 50 homes, catalogue more than 1,500 items, and record almost 100 hours of oral history. Three years of work resulted in an exhibition of which Annie is still proud. "I love being a Canadian. I'm deeply proud of this country, and I'm very determined.

"I love a challenge, which is why Inventive Women appeals to me, since it is uncharted territory," she says. "I'm fascinated by the changes our world is experiencing as a result of the emergence of the technology age. Neat stuff. And I want to be a part of it."

Evelyn Hannon

Creator
Journeywoman
www.journeywoman.com

Back in 1982, divorced and alone for the first time in her
life, Evelyn Hannon experienced a range of emotions. Fear
was high the list. Fear of being alone. Fear of traveling
alone. Fear of everyday failures on a small and grand scale.
So at age 42, she decided to tackle one of those fears: she
bought a backpack and set out on a five-week journey. On
her own.

For 35 days in Europe, Evelyn—a mother of two talented
daughters—was completely independent for the first time in
many years. Asked to recall that sojourn, she remembers
laughter and tears and the decision to force herself to be a
part of the larger world. In 35 days, she ate only five
dinners alone. Her travels, then and since, have helped
Evelyn build connections with women in myriad cities and

countries; along the way, she
discovered things of practical
value to travelers, especially
single travelers and women travelers—gems like which super-
markets to shop at in a foreign
city; where to find a local female
doctor; where to buy underwear;
which areas of a city to avoid
after dark; and the names of

TIM LEYES

modest neighborhood restaurants where a woman dining alone won't be hassled.

Evelyn filled notebooks with observations on that first trip. It was, she observes with hindsight, the beginning of an informal network connecting traveling women around the world. In 1994, she sat down and wrote a 24-page newsletter, self-published it, and named it Journeywoman. She decided to make it a quarterly publication. Faxes requesting subscriptions arrived from all over the world. "Soon," says Evelyn, "Journeywoman was being read by 6,000 women travelers, internationally . . . Without knowing it, I'd tapped into a vast niche market—females who love to travel."

Journeywoman was written up in more than 100 publications around the world. Advertisers signed on. "Journeywoman," she says, "was growing faster than I could work. I no longer had time to travel." Evelyn knew little about cyberspace, but gradually realized that publishing her newsletter on the Web might be the way to go. "Since my mandate was to inspire women

---

Try the transportation...

First and foremost, learn how to get around on your own. Try the transportation. Hop a double-decker streetcar as it makes its way from one end of HK Island to the other. If you see something you absolutely love, get off and explore.

Then, test the spotless **Hong Kong MTR** (subway system) designed with female safety in mind. This immaculately clean system is well lit and constantly monitored by the railway police and MTR staff. Within the subway cars women are protected from potential trouble as open-ended cars allow for free movement throughout the train. Someone bothering you? Just move to the next compartment. How's that for female-friendly transportation?

Excerpt from
www. journeywoman.com

---

to travel safely and well, and to connect female travelers internationally, what better way than to use the Internet?"

She was nagged by an obvious, practical problem: who'd pay the bills when readers were no longer paying for subscriptions? Advertisers? Sponsors? Despite the uncertainty, Evelyn took a leap of faith: "I had to believe that if my readership became large enough, the financial support would eventually come." Knowing nothing about how to build or launch a Web site, she hired "a wonderful Webmaster and cyber technician," Iain Smy, who helped her translate into design and graphics Journeywoman's online presence.

"In a way, perhaps being a novice helped me to design a site where all women, even women with little experience, could navigate easily and could feel at home. I kept the size of the font large enough so that it could be read by anybody of any age. Color was kept to a minimum. The site had to load easily and quickly. That meant no travel photos. I would offer bold, black, line drawings and cartoons that would stimulate the reader's imagination. In terms of content, I included categories designed to make any traveling female's heart sing—features such as solo travel trips, eco adventures, spa stories, female-friendly city sites, where to find a doctor, tips on what to wear, where to dine if you're traveling alone—all the things that I looked for when I first started traveling solo, and had no mentors to teach me."

Anybody can visit the site free of charge, leave some advice, and benefit from the thousands of tips and stories already posted there. At the time of writing, well over half a million surfers had visited the site, and insurance and travel companies had signed on as clients. At the Journeywoman home page, readers are given the option of subscribing to Journeywoman Online, a free quarterly email newsletter that includes the top travel tips sent to the site. A "baby-sister" site, HERmail.net, is a directory listing female travelers around the world. A traveler setting off on a journey can make Internet contact with other females at her destination. Evelyn celebrated her 58th birthday by hiking in the Red Mountains, reporting from Oprah Winfrey's favorite café in Chicago, slipping into a thermal spa in Tuscany. Now, she's taking another step. Her award-winning Web site is being turned into a documentary-style television series. Evelyn's two daughters, Erica and Leslie, are working with their mother on this new venture. "The same daughters who used to tell me I was technologically challenged."

Carly Milne

Editor and Publisher
Moxie
www.moxie.ca

Carly Milne's hair, swept up, reveals a tattoo on the side of her neck, a clue about the creator of Moxie.ca, the popular online network made for, and by, women. The dictionary reveals another: "**Moxie:** Slang. The ability to face difficulty with spirit."

"I actually didn't go to school," she says. "I started writing young."

Carly nailed her first professional gig at 14, writing for a Canadian newspaper. She'd dropped out of high school and had started pounding the pavement, looking for work—learning by the "hand-on-the-burner" method is the way she puts it.

Carly's no stranger to scars: her parents divorced when she was five. She was bounced back and forth between cities and parents until the age of 13, surviving emotional, physical, and sexual abuse. At 15, she was out on her own. By 20, Carly had discovered two things: she could drink and she could write. She recalls

KEN EAKIN, 1999

being in class, useless and intoxicated; at the same time, she was a regular contributor to her school newspaper, *The Scarlet Fever*, which that year claimed an award as North America's best high school newspaper.

"Writing was my salvation during that period," Carly told *Gomagazine* in a 1999 interview. "I was really messed up and . . . I had never felt so unloved and out of control."

A teacher encouraged her to contact the local daily newspaper, where she landed a job and started stirring up reaction as a teen-page columnist who tackled such messy, real-life issues as divorce and safe sex. Then the Internet became alive to her; she saw a world of new-media possibilities. The concept for Moxie came to her after she landed an editorial job with the Canadian version of the U.S. search engine and portal Yahoo! Disappointed in her online hunt for women-oriented sites, she decided to create the site for which she was fruitlessly searching—something written by women, for women, with a Canadian focus. Carly started tracking down people she felt personified the Moxie spirit; through friends, associates, and groups such as Toronto's Webgrrls [www.torontowebgrrls.com], she began pooling resources and contracting Web design firms.

The hardest part was convincing women to invest time and money to create a corner of the Web they could call their own. But invest they did. Why? Because Moxie filled a specific, demographic niche. Written by women, for women, it profiles Canadian women who have the power to lead and inspire; it delivers articles, forums, and "femme-friendly links"; it offers a range of sites, such as music reviews from *Sway Magazine*, jock talk from *Sportsfemmes*, and essays on sex, sexuality, gender, and body issues from *Sins*.

The Moxie team is constantly working on building new sites, and those who want their site to be part of Moxie must go through "an intense process," says Milne: subject criteria must be well defined; the site must be professionally designed and updated frequently. Moxie reflects Carly's feminist philosophy as well as her desire to create an open, inclusive space.

As editor, publisher, "and general mucky-muck," Carly is headmistress of three ezines and one portal. For the ezines, she assigns and edit articles, writes and edits her own articles, monitors message boards, updates sites, and handles promotion via search engines, reciprocal links, and press releases. For the portal, she gather info from all sites for inclusion in a weekly newsletter she writes; Carly also monitors message boards, edits, and assigns for Moxie Chick and Woman profiles.

She works at least 8 to 10 hours a day and "often, a bit more. I get in this zone where I have no concept of time and I just keep going." She's one in a group of women who have endeavored to make the Net a more women-friendly place. The world of new media—and online publishing—is a fresh frontier, an interactive medium where collaboration, ambition, and support can collide. Even, sometimes, create something inspirational.

Carly raises a hand and touches the tattoo on her neck. When asked about its significance, she explains it's the Chinese symbol for "Danger." "I was inspired by the Chinese proverb 'Where there is danger, there is opportunity.'"

On the tender, inside curve of her right arm, just below the elbow, is another tattoo, this time the symbol for "Strength." It's "to commemorate my survival of a form of chemo. They took blood from that spot every week."

The symbol for "Courage" is on her left foot, commemorating the launch of Moxie.ca. Her back bears a final symbol, a Chinese character that's hard to define. It can mean several things. "Ambition. Truth," says Carly. "Destiny. Energy."

And now, "Moxie."

Jennifer Corriero, Tsipora Mankovsky, and Tania Botticella

Coolgirls Creators
www.coolgirls.net

Jennifer Corriero, Tsipora Mankovsky, and Tania Botticella are the teen creators of **Coolgirls.net**, a Web site aimed at inspiring a whole generation of girls. Coolgirls is a virtual community where girls can learn about women's history (herstory) and connect with each other about important issues that are relevant to their own lives. The site's motto: "The past has everything to do with the present. Everything is connected."

Coolgirls.net is the daughter site of Coolwomen.org. Tania describes their relationship: "Coolwomen has a very 'feminist' perspective on everything. At Coolgirls, we just talk about life." And talk, they do . . . about anything and everything including life, love, relationships, dreams, fears, hopes, and, oh, yeah—technology. A lot of people have written to the site expressing their gratitude at being part of "a forum to unleash opinions . . . a place where young voices can be heard."

At 19, Tania has already been working in new media for almost two years. The self-professed "child of technology" never imagined she would have the opportunity to create the kinds of projects and gain the experience she has in such a short time. Her passion for writing drew her to the Web when she realized the Internet offered a unique outlet of expression and a wealth of potential career opportunities. "I love to write and I believe that you should study and work by doing what you love. School doesn't get you a job: your ambition does."

Tania's personal ambition for Coolgirls is "to provoke deep analysis about the world around us and to network with people of all ages."

Jennifer Corriero, who is also 19 and serves as the site's project manager, says Coolgirls is a forum to provoke awareness, analysis, exploration, growth, initiative, and change, while encouraging people to take pride in who they were, are, and will create. She acknowledges the inherent value of constructing the site when she says, "This challenging experience has given me a glimpse at my own potential. Not only have I gained insight into my dreams and my goals, I have come to understand how to surpass the limits that I place on myself."

At 17, Tsipora Mankovsky is the youngest Coolgirl, yet she already has a wealth of personal insight. She has been dabbling in new media since she was 14 and her responsibilities at Coolgirls include graphic design, writing poetry, collecting artwork, and handling publicity. "It says 'Visioneer' on my business card . . . I guess that's a role and a responsibility—thinking big." And Tsipora tends to think bigger than most young women her age. Her life ambition is "to change the world."

And her ambition for Coolgirls is "to create an open and honest forum for girls to express themselves in different ways and at the same time see how their expressions relate to past expression done by other women." In other words, you can be yourself and at the same time connect to a rich history of "women who thought some of the same things as you, dreamt some of the same things as you. I think it's about appreciating the struggles of the past, building bridges to understand yourself and the world you live in . . . and to see examples of women who have created their own world and existence through dreams, struggles, strengths, and love. This, to me, is very powerful."

The teen trio also has very explicit opinions about technology, its value, and its potential. "Technology is really of no consequence to me. What is of consequence, however, is how we use it and how we recognize its power and the division of that power." Tsipora agrees: "I was not and never will be interested in technology. I care about people, their lives, their culture, their practices, their organizations, change. I'm only interested in what it can do."

The girls perhaps best express their newly gained self-confidence in their own potential through their self-appointed titles. Tania chose Content Engineer as her career calling card, while Jennifer adopted Chief Energizer. Tsipora, formerly known as a Passion Architect, now prefers to be called Visioneer. Each title reflects an awareness of the teen's personal skill set and clearly puts technology in the backdrop where they feel it belongs.

The girls had to overcome their own intimidation of technology in order to realize its potential. Jennifer remembers the watershed day when the Coolgirls first formed as a team: "I kept asking, 'Who's the techie? Who's the techie?' Our focus was never on the technical part of the project.

Our focus was on ourselves and our message. Technology was just the tool to build our vision."

So what do these tech-savvy girls most fear about technology now that they have each conquered their personal challenges in facing it? Tsipora's greatest fear was that technology is currently taking over people's lives and that "people forget that it is a tool and that it should strive to enrich culture and community and not snuff it. But I guess that's not really a fear about technology. Technology can't do that . . . *people* do that."

Jennifer acknowledges that she "feared technology and saw it as a block, rather than a door. Really, it's an avenue for me to express my ideas, have them heard, and network with people from all over the world."

Asked how the invention of Coolgirls has affected their lives, all three girls are quick to defend the process of the creation rather than the final outcome. Tsipora explains: "Coolgirls didn't make a difference. Putting together a fabulous Web site from scratch, working with the girls, listening to women's stories, pushing ourselves to go further, building relationships with Coolwomen, learning from them (they're all wise jewels!)—that made the difference."

Tania agrees: "It's not the product, but rather how we got there: the struggle we encountered; the success we attained; the foundation for our futures that we have built. Coolgirls gave me the chance to fail. It also taught me about the importance of giving people opportunities to learn and fail. We failed so many times before we succeeded."

For Jennifer it was also a personal success: "Coolgirls has empowered me to believe in my potential, and to recognize that the possibilities are limitless! Many people have said that our site is inspiring, whether it be through the stories that are told, the artwork that is showcased, or the opportunity that we give to express and connect. I believe that we have created something very powerful."

Powerful, indeed. The "cool girl" inventors are poised to bring themselves and their entire generation into the digital millennium.

When Anita Borg told a respected colleague she'd established an experimental R&D institute for women and technology, his negative response floored her—and led to a professional epiphany: "Men just assume they're designing technology that's for everybody. Because most of the people making our high-tech tools are male, technology primarily reflects men's needs and perspectives, or men's perceptions of women's needs." Today, she's at work at her institute, developing technology that works with women's lives. Her latest project? A family computer.

Modern technology extends our levels of comfort, our professional curiosity, even our human life spans. Still, something's missing. "If women designed cars, there'd be a place for a purse," says Dr. Anita Borg. This line cracks her

up: she heard it this morning at a conference she's attending, and this afternoon it still resonates. "Well, think about it. For 35 years, I've been getting into a car. Putting [my purse] behind the seat and you can't reach it." The end of the sentence is lost in laughter.

It's a funny thing, watching an acclaimed computer scientist lose herself in laughter. Anita is a pioneer in work on fault-tolerant operating systems. She's developed tools to predict the performance of microprocessor memory systems. And she has a sense of humor, especially in the face of absurdity.

Anita's world is ringed by engineers and computer scientists. She's damn smart: great grades and glowing recommendations from professors paved the way for a full scholarship when she went after her PhD in computer science at New York University. Still, it took her a while to figure some things out: for instance, she didn't realize until she was in her forties that women are "professional schizophrenics."

"I mean, at work, you leave the woman part at home; at home, you leave the confident engineer part at work; female engineers usually leave the female part out of the equation. It's not just the technical field. But I think it's kind of extreme in the technical field," she says. "And it's a shame because, what it winds up meaning, is that all the sources of inspiration that come from women's experience are less [influential]. Things get categorized as 'women's stuff,' and you don't feel comfortable bringing it into the equation. And, when you think about it, 'women's stuff' is half the stuff!" Another peal of laughter and this time Anita's earrings, which dangle below her earlobes, ricochet in response.

Fear, however, seems to be at the heart of this woman's forcefulness. Not fear of the usual stuff. Loneliness or financial insecurity or heights or speed. She can white-water kayak, pilot a Cessna, commit to a marriage. That line about cars and purses resonates with her because it goes to the heart of what Anita hates, and fears, the most: she hates that women have been left out of technology's research and development. What if only 30-year-old women developed technology, and it was geared mainly to the consumer appetites of 13-year-old girls? That's the reality of the world in which we now live, she says: men hold the power, and boys drive the market.

And her fears center on technology's undemocratic evolution, and how this gap will shape our future. Look around you, she says. Who hold the high-ranking corporate posts in technology companies? Who are filling most of the seats in computer science and engineering classes? If women aren't at the beginning or the end of that technological food chain, they are not influencing the equation. Whether our new digital tools reflect women's needs depends on the extent to which women are involved in technological development, and the extent to which their needs are taken into account.

Anita asks us to consider the shape, the size, the function, and the user interfaces of technological creations. Every invention reflects the values, perspective, background, and needs of its inventor. It wasn't until women started flooding into medical schools that the medical profession began questioning whether research using only male subjects was applicable to women. If this inequity in technology's influence and evolution never really occurred to you, don't feel bad: Anita says it took her a while to realize that technology is not neutral and that its development is not democratic. She recalls that when she decided to found an institute for women and technology, she mentioned it to a colleague. "This man, who is head of the school of computer science at a prestigious American university, is a very nice man, and really understands that the culture in this school's computer science program is very narrow and needs to be opened up somehow. I told him about the institute. And I said that one thing that you can do is try to bring inspiration to technology from women's situations.

"And he stopped for a second and said, 'Hmm. Women and technology? Isn't that awfully narrow?'" Anita stops and looks at me, searching for some indication of recognition and empathy. Her eyes seem to say: *Can you imagine how hard I've worked to get backing for the idea of this institute? Can you imagine how I felt when someone I respected had this response to all my efforts?*

As the conversation flows, it turns to products. Stoves designed by men, which can't be cleaned. Copiers and printers and office equipment that aren't sized to women, although women tend to be their majority users. Pagers, cell phones, and Palm Pilots. The way many of these technological creations are designed doesn't reflect women's wants or needs. Anita likes to point out how Palm Pilots are designed with cases that strap onto belts, yet women carry PDAs—Personal Digital Assistants—in purses. (Then throw their purses . . . somewhere in the car.)

She cofounded the Institute for Women and Technology (IWT) in 1997 to persuade companies to consider the female perspective when designing high-tech tools, and to get more women involved in creating them. The non-profit organization is housed at Xerox's Palo Alto Research Center (PARC), a place Anita describes as a boiling pot of innovation. Back in the 1970s, Xerox PARC was the hottest research facility in computing; the first real personal computer, the Alto, was created there. Like the engineering world, PARC is traditionally a boys' club but Anita says when she approached the center's senior players—ubiquitous computing guru Mark Weiser and PARC director John Seely Brown—they opened their doors and offered the support required to get her center rolling. "They've brought in artists, all sorts of different kinds of people. They realize that it's still mostly male and they are willing to give some support to the idea that to bring women's perspectives in, in a different way, could really [enrich] their innovative engine."

Now, women in her IWT brainstorming sessions are looking at products. What about smart pipes that warn homeowners if a pipe is about to freeze, clog, or leak? Or a virtual wall that lets grandma "sit" with her grandchildren in another city? Swivelling car seats that make access easier for physically challenged folks? Security devices that let kids signal if they're in danger? The IWT is persuading companies to consider the female perspective when they shape our "everyday" technology, and getting more women involved in their creation. The IWT's workshops, Internet technology communities, publications, programs and conferences are all geared to this mandate, and its Virtual Development Centre connects business, community, and academia in Internet-based, collaborative environments to development designs and prototypes based on input from women.

"All over this country, there are projects looking at technology for the home with very few or no women involved. So the idea was to turn that on its head," she says. "And think of it from the perspective of the people in the home, or the extended family, or whatever people define as families—whatever their personal family experience is." Participants in the IWT's experimental workshops are from technical and non-technical fields. They are mothers, wives, daughters, sisters. The age range at the first workshop stretched from 13 to 72. Anita invited her 72-year-old mother, an artist, and her sister, whom she describes as "somewhere between a full-time skier and a house builder." Neither uses computers.

"The idea is to get a diverse group of people together to look at a broad topic like technology in support of families and see if we can, from the personal experiences of the people who participate, get an understanding of what would really be useful to them.

"I was so proud of my mother," Anita recalls. The woman billed as a Silicon Valley superstar had never really talked to her mother about her work. Her mother's response to what she saw, to this window on the world of interactive technology and accessible online information, was to offer a very practical suggestion: she asked her daughter, the legendary computer scientist, two simple questions: "Not everybody goes into some room with their own computer so why can't we have something that allows us to use all this information that is out there as a family, together? Why couldn't we do that, and do it in connection with your cousin's family in Alabama?"

Anita finds it fascinating that women continually mention "this notion of using stuff together" because she believes that feminine instinct to collaborate and network is "a key influence."

"I think that we have an opportunity to shift our thinking from the very individualist way of looking at computers and information technology to one which takes into account, in much richer ways, the social relationships that we hold dear. Often, non-technical people perceive technology as products and systems that break down our social fabric and isolate us." Anita's response? Don't damn the technology. Think about it, together. Great tools can be conceived and constructed so that they "support and enrich those things we hold dear," rather than threaten them, she says.

"I have this idea." The subject animates Anita's body and she hunches forward, over the coffee table. "We could be sitting here, having this conversation and we could—" Her hand plunks down some imaginary bauble on the table between us. "We could have something small here. This thing could become a participant in our discussion in a way that we could interact with it. It would be, say, connected to the Internet, or whatever, and as we discussed things, it might feed us with information." She pauses. Briefly lost in her vision, Anita looks up from the invisible invention on the table. "It might key in on what we are talking about and go searching for things that are relevant. Or we could turn to it and say: 'Who has done stuff like this already?' And rather than us having to interact through the computer, we interact together. With it. It becomes a kind of participant. In our conversation."

We run with Anita's idea. So what we have on the table before us is a portable, technological accessory to our conversation—something that integrates into, and facilitates our exchange, without dominating the agenda or isolating us physically? "Right!" she says. A huge grin. "And it doesn't drive people apart. It enhances people being together. I mean, all of the work—most of the work—that's been done on technologies to support work groups and social groups assumes that people are not co-operative. Or that even if they are [co-operative], these technologies are created with the assumption that people must then go off into their own offices and only interact with each other via computer. So, then, that computer intermediates. Which is great when people are far apart. But when they are not, it doesn't make sense."

Women are not enamored of technology for technology's sake. Women are practical, they want service, she says. And if companies start paying attention to that distinction, "and really start figuring out how to push that all the way back into the technology development piece, that will be interesting."

This approach is starting to make sense to some of the world's most powerful technology companies. Companies such as IBM are figuring out how to change their relationship with female customers. And, along with Hewlett-Packard, Sun Microsystems, Xerox Corporation, Compaq Corporation, and others, they are helping fund and support the IWT's research and development.

Xerox's research center is a perfect place for Anita, who's

used to both creating and solving problems. Among her creations is Systers, one of the world's oldest global electronic networks of women in computer science, connecting more than 2,500 women in 25 countries. She also cofounded the Grace Hopper Celebration of Women in Computing, a prestigious conference for women in computer science.

Anita's after a broader, richer technology—one that reflects a more humanistic perspective in the way it's used. That kind of technology opens the door for women to bring their whole selves to the job. And it will do the same thing for men: it will open up areas of richness and avenues of creativity and collaboration, she says. But first, we need more female engineers shaping and designing the technology that's shaping our lives.

Women have increasingly assumed their role and their responsibility in the political arena over the past 20 years; over the next 20 years, technology will change our political, economic, social, and personal landscapes. Women need to assume responsibility for our digital lives. The way Anita sees it, if tomorrow is to be different from today, women must say: "This is how we want to change things."

Scarlet Pollock and Jo Sutton

Activists, Cofounders
Women'space
www.womenspace.ca

Jo Sutton and Scarlet Pollock are online activists. From their rural Ontario home, they are linked to a global feminist network they helped to create, and are devoted to projects involving women and information/communications technology. *Women'space* was cofounded by Jo and Scarlet in 1995 as a quarterly print magazine and eventually expanded into a women's online network, an evolution sparked by the magazine's key volunteers (Jo, Scarlet, Penney Kome, Denise Osted, Juliet Breese, and Judy Michaud) and contributing writers, all of whom were early explorers of women's sites online. Today, *Women'space* has blossomed into a print magazine, a listserv, and a nonprofit organization focused on promoting women's equality through Internet use and awareness. We reached

Jo and Scarlet via email, naturally, to ask how they began this online community and to shed some light on their lives as activists in a wired world.

The pair first connected with women who were already online in 1995. Supported and encouraged by that inter-action, they started a Web site. "Virtual Sisterhood, a women's electronic strategy group, took our work to the Beijing women's conference in August/September 1995, which gave Women'space some international visibility," says Jo. "Denise, Judy, and Penney joined soon after, providing a network across Canada."

The Women'space mailing list was actually suggested by the women's caucus at a 1996 conference—Getting Online: Communities on the Internet—and, activists say, the listserv has grown because that's what women want to join. Jo and Scarlet try to take a hands-off approach, letting people raise issues of most concern to them. "Sometimes we raise issues and facilitate specific discussions on the mailing list. Personal email has also contributed to the online community. Some-times we use it to support women's contributions to the list; we sometimes follow up on issues raised on the list. Our Out Box is about 30 emails a day, with about 25 individu-ally written. By this time there were many women we had met online, but had never seen face to face."

With federal funding, Women'space coordinated a Women's Internet Conference in 1997, "which hit the ground running because so many women who attended already knew each other virtually, via email and Web sites," says Jo, adding that the conference proved to be an effective venue for networking, collaboration, and—ultimately—lobbying for change.

The Canadian government has, so far, been "incredibly boneheaded" about doing a gender-based analysis of the Connecting Canadians programs, they say, referring to the federal initiative aimed at making Canada the most connected country in the world by the year 2000. From that initiative sprang VolNet, the Voluntary Network Support Program aimed at bringing Canada's voluntary sector online. (The Canadian government earmarked $15 million for the effort in the February 1998 federal budget, with the goal of connecting 10,000 volunteer organizations to the Internet by the end of fiscal year 2000.)

"There is widespread anger in women's groups about [their] exclusion from government programs that are spending hundreds of millions of dollars," says Jo, who notes that lobby pressure in the wake of their 1997 Women's Internet Conference launched three women onto the federal government committee, which in turn resulted in VolNet. "Web sites increase visibility and transparency. It's a place for information, sharing experiences, visions, and the achievements of women activists online, and another route for people to connect with us." It's also "a form of pressure," she says. "The analysis of the Canadian government's treatment of nonprofit women's groups and ICT (Information/Communications Technology) is a very public statement which is an irritant to government, and which we hope will be part of the array of ways we put pressure on for improvement."

Most of the women who make up *Women'space*'s online community are feminist activists representing a wide range of women and women's groups, including women with disabilities, women who are immigrants, and lesbians. "A few academics," says Jo. "And both rural and urban women are involved. The concentrated portion are in Canada, but there are also women from across the world participating."

Was the global listserv/Web site/magazine born of a desire to encourage this community to explore the power they can generate through their use of information technology? "The short answer is 'yes,'" says Jo. "We're so impressed by the creativity, imagination, skills, and hard work of women online. We love working with them. Online activism is still developing, and we love how far we can reach, how much we can discover and learn, and that we can let our imaginations run wild with ideas how to apply the technology for equality."

In the online *Women'space* essay "Information Technology Is a Women's Rights Issue," Jo and Scarlet jointly express their specific concerns about access: namely that women do not gain access to public resources on an equal basis with men, including access to the new information technologies. They started out, online, with pure enthusiasm and a desire to share "this neat, new form of communicating with others," says Jo. They grew to realize that access is a many faceted issue. "It's about income, education, opportunity, and openness to new ideas. We've learned a great deal from conversations with many women, from women's Web sites, books, and articles," says Jo, adding that the duo's "paid work" is to press for access, improved access, appropriate access, cheap access, and safe access. "Early on, we realized that women tend to not get online just because it's there. There has to be a reason to get online. So we believe you can't have access without a purpose: emailing with the kids when they leave home (or the kids emailing home for money), wanting to connect with others enduring the same health problem, sharing life experiences, finding information, working for change."

Are they, ultimately, optimistic that concerns regarding access will be addressed? "Yes and no. People with sufficient money will get online, just like people got TVs in the fifties and sixties. Most kids will grow up wondering what the world was like before the Internet. All Canada's schools are wired, and now the government is planning to wire most classrooms. But there is a problem for people on low incomes, a group that is disproportionately women. It will be a disadvantage to not have a computer at home, because that's where you will get much of your information—and hopefully also create it. If access is [about] getting online to buy something, or to find a government form, then it's less of a problem. If access is civic participation, the building of an inclusive, democratic and interactive society, then we have a long way to go. Obviously, we're in favor of the second model."

Jo says that, as she types the above thought, she can look out of a north-facing window ("less glare on the screen") and see a forest of bare maple trees, rocks, and the patch that she hopes will grow the bulbs she planted last fall. Life continues, both online and off, as digital and real worlds merge. "The dogs are tumbling over each other in the snow and I know they'll soon want to come in and drip around my feet. We tend to use a Pentium 133 for work, with its nearly full 2 GB hard drive. There's a P450 in the kitchen, 13 GB hard drive, but when you use that [computer], our 21-month-old daughter climbs up into a lap and expects her programs to appear."

Betty Hall
Active Online

Friday, January 7, 2000

I turned on my computer at 7:30 and connected to my Internet service provider to access Web Broker to make a couple of trades on the Toronto Stock Exchange.

After that I read my email. There was a letter from my brother who lives in Ann Arbor, Michigan, asking for a photo that I had taken with my digital camera last summer. In a matter of a few minutes, I answered him and sent the picture by email.

I also had mail from the *Economist*, who I've asked to send me their "business and politics in brief" articles.

Before disconnecting from the Internet, I went to a site that I have bookmarked to read the daily press releases from various companies. My self-administered RRIF account is rather conservative, and I don't make many trades, but with my Greenline account I do, and have had a lot of success (and fun) with it.

Later in the morning, I had a meeting with our Life-Long Learning Program committee, but I couldn't wait to get home to find out if my trades on the stock market had gone through at the prices that I had requested. They had. Then I checked my two portfolios,

Canoe.ca and Quicken.ca, to see how they were doing. On both these sites I have entered the stocks that I own, the price I paid for them, and the date they were purchased. Both sites, with only a 15- or 20-minute delay, constantly update the current prices and performance, which means I can always stay up to date. I

Seniors on the Internet

Although the Internet revolution is often perceived as a youth movement, nothing could be further from the truth. Older adults are one of the fastest growing demographics online. In 1995 just 600,000 were online (SeniorNet, 1995), but that number had reached 13 million by 1998 (Neilson Media, 1998). Not only are older adults coming online in droves, but they also spend more time online and are more likely to make a purchase online than any other age group (Harris, 1998).

also quickly checked my bank and other accounts through Web banking, and paid my outstanding bills.

Recently, I contacted Canada Post about their new EPOST service and arranged to have any bills I would ordinarily receive through regular mail sent to that site. Also, any deposits to my bank account, e.g., Old Age Pension, are automatically deposited. I also pay my quarterly income tax via Web banking and now can send my income tax return from home via email (NetFile).

This afternoon I will download from my camera the pictures that I took over the holidays of my grandchildren. I'll put them into my album with Photo Organizer, and some will also go in my Family Tree Maker, which has a scrapbook for every member of the family. This Christmas I transferred some pictures I'd taken in the summer onto T-shirts for my sons and sons-in-law. I had fun doing it, and the T-shirts made great, inexpensive presents.

All these photographs take up a lot of space, so about a year ago I bought a new Dell Computer with a DVD CD-ROM, a 19-inch monitor, and lots of memory. It's great for watching DVD movies! Since then I have had installed a Recordable CD Drive so that I can make copies of pictures in case something goes wrong with my hard drive. I don't usually print out my pictures, but keep them all on my computer, unless I use them to make birthday cards or other gifts. I can also use them to put together some great slide shows for my family.

Some days (especially at Christmas time) I shop on the Internet, mostly at Chapters for books, but also at toy stores if I'm shopping for my grandchildren. On other days I might click on an icon I have on my desktop that says Collingwood Library. I can get into the library catalog and put books on hold; the library phones me when they are in, and I can go and pick up the books I reserved. Perhaps one day they'll be able to email me instead of calling!

At the end of the day I write in my diary. I have kept this daily since I was 50, 26 years ago, and for the past 11 of these 26 years I've kept my diary on my computer. It's very handy to be able to search for what you did on a certain date or at a certain place.

I also update my Quicken account with any VISA purchases or bills paid from that day.

If I have time, I might go to the Ski Canada Web site to check in on how my grandchildren are doing in their ski races. (Of course, I also like to watch them on the hills, and ski with them on occasion.)

Having a computer is not only a lot of fun, but also has freed up time for me to spend reading, walking,

So what is drawing older adults to the Internet? According to recent research by SeniorNet (1998) most older adults use the Internet to communicate with friends and family. The second most popular activity is research and accessing news and current events. Older adults use the Internet in much the same way as younger folks for communication and information, and they are very much a part of the new Internet age.

Ann Wrixon
President & CEO
SeniorNet
www.seniornet.org

and skiing. I feel very grateful to my children for buying me my first computer in 1988, a color printer in 1993, and my digital camera in 1998. I can't believe how organized I am, thanks to this computer.

Sally Burch

Online Activist
http://alainet.org

Sally Burch is a concerned digital citizen. As an online activist based in Quito, Ecuador, she is committed to bridging the global gap between haves and have-nots when it comes to Information and Communication Technologies (ICTs). Thanks to email and online discussion groups, women from all over the world are beginning to connect around important topics such as access. Sally says the electronic discussion groups she helps to moderate have become the backbone of the advocacy movement. "Before email, an exchange of this kind would have been unthinkable without a face-to-face meeting. In fact, in the recent past, women in the South would have been generally excluded from participation in this sort of exchange at all. Now, as long as we have access to the technology, it is relatively easy to have a voice in this kind of forum from anywhere in the world. Of course, we know that we are still a privileged minority."

Sally runs a nonprofit communications organization called *Agencia Latinoamericana de Informacion* (ALAI), which is dedicated to democratizing communication and to supporting the communication initiatives of social movements. Her organization provides information channels (Internet and print) and training so that women and nonprofit groups can engage in advocacy around communication policy issues.

As a woman living in Ecuador, Sally, 50, fully understands the importance of the Internet for connecting and communicating. "Since we are working in a communications program in the international sphere, from a country with a precarious communications system, the Internet (basically email) has been fundamental to improving the possibilities of communicating." Since the Internet has been their only means to network without the need to centralize, her group has taken an active role in promoting the use of electronic networks for social networking, not only in Ecuador but throughout South America. As a result, ALAI's efforts have made a huge difference in how Latin American organizations interconnect and organize.

For example, Sally was formerly the coordinator of the APC Women's Networking Support Program [**www.gn.apc.org/apcwomen/**], a worldwide initiative that promotes women's access to and use of the Internet. The context was the preparation for the 4th World Conference on Women (Beijing, 1995), in which the program played a significant role in helping women's organizations get connected to the Internet and use it strategically to network and exchange information. The program also played a key role in getting information to countries that are normally isolated from the already "connected circles." Since then, APC and ALAI have joined other organizations in building the WomenAction 2000 global initiative [**www.women-action.org**], a network of organizations from all over the world with the common goal of enabling NGOs to actively engage in the "Beijing+5" dynamic (a review process taking place five years after the Beijing women's conference).

For Sally, participation in such networks as these means her work in the field of gender and communication has a broader scope and greater impact. She also recognizes the potential value of the Internet as an important and potentially transformative tool. "If women and other marginalized social groups do not gain today the know-how and training to take advantage of and make their mark on this new medium, their exclusion is likely to be even deeper in the near future."

As an Ecuadorian resident, Sally also realizes that ICT development is clearly controlled by the North, mainly by the U.S., and, therefore, can vouch for the fact that women from other countries have even fewer possibilities than their northern counterparts to have a say in that process. Nonetheless, she claims that some women's organizations, in Africa for example, have been urging their governments to develop a national policy for ICT development and to incorporate a gender focus. But Sally is quick to note that women in rural areas of the North also have access problems, since, currently, most digitized broadband highways are concentrated in business districts of major cities. These are just a few of the access issues that are on the table for women's movements around the world, and organizations like Sally's ALAI are leading the way in educating and encouraging women to take action.

Women like Sally are banding together globally to take up the rallying cry for access to and inclusion in any and all discussions focused on the future shaping of the Internet, as well as challenging any proprietary ownership of knowledge. Sally is the first to remind us of the importance for all debate to begin with discussion. "We as women must define what our needs are as women and as citizens." Through Sally's efforts, women are beginning to listen and, perhaps more importantly, ensure that everyone has a voice.

Lynda Leonard

Vice President, Communications
Information Technology Association of Canada (ITAC)
www.itac.ca

Lynda Leonard is a mother of three, a brave change agent, a Tank Girl aficionado, and a tireless technology advocate.

Since 1977 Lynda has been artfully combining her passion for technology with her communications prowess, beginning with a position as manager, public relations, for the TransCanada Telephone System. Having always been an avid reader and writer, and having studied arts and journalism at university, Lynda landed the TransCanada Telephone job, her first technology-related position, by practicing her craft. She had been hired to write a story for *Reader's Digest* called "10 Ways to Cut Your Phone Bill." Going from company to company to conduct research, Lynda met interesting people in the telecommunications business, and before she knew it, her interview subjects had become her colleagues.

But her real road-to-Damascus experience came in 1991 when she began to see some of the earliest applications of interactive multimedia. When she saw a South African activist explaining how a simple computer application was improving educational opportunities in remote villages, Lynda felt sure she was seeing the future. Not only that, but she realized she wanted that future now, so she decided to dedicate her talents to making that vision of the future a reality.

Lynda got well and truly hooked on technology when she watched kids in Newfoundland connecting via Schoolnet to kids in the N'sga valley. They used technology to learn about life in each other's communities without a textbook or even a teacher. And then Lynda started connecting with technology herself, learning to wash lettuce with Julia Child on CD, and understanding that computers and technology were tools that could help her to explore the things she cared about.

> "I never feel out of place at work, but I do I feel like an 'interruption'—my gender is like a visa permitting me to be different, introduce new ideas, and challenge complacency. I think it's a lot harder for men to be agents of change."

Today Lynda is the vice president, communications, for ITAC—the Information Technology Association of Canada. Using an array of digital and analogue tools to spur the growth of the IT industry in Canada, she enjoys being a technology advocate. She works closely with ITAC's members to help bring Canada closer to becoming a comprehensive knowledge-based economy, and claims that her greatest challenge at work is staying hip and avoiding complacency.

But staying hip to technology and the new wired culture seems to come naturally to Lynda, and as an outspoken technology user, she is in no danger of being called complacent. She speaks her mind, pushes the envelope, and shares her knowledge and time generously to advance other people's love of technology.

Whether it's changing the world or scouring eBay for Tank Girl paraphernalia, Lynda is always firm in her belief that technology can bring positive benefits to our communities and lives. As a player in the public policy environment, Lynda works to ensure the climate in Canada fosters innovation and knowledge creation. Combine that commitment to serious change with the pure sense of fun she derives from technology success stories, and you have the perfect advocate.

Esther Dyson
"A Net Architect's New Vistas"

www.edventure.com

The daughter of a Swiss mathematician mother and a physicist father, Esther Dyson is a digital architect. A friend of Bill Gates, she has the ear of presidents and prime ministers. An online presence before most of today's dotcom millionaires and billionaires ever heard of email, Esther says the Internet is tailor-made to help women finally find their voices—and to shift the traditional balance of power.

How much influence can one voice have in the digital landscape? Consider Esther Dyson. While it's hard to pin one professional label on her, it's easy to appreciate Esther's singular influence, online and off. "I'm diversified," she says. "Like the Internet." In her previous professional incarnations she's been a Wall Street securities analyst, a reporter

for *Forbes* magazine, chair of the Electronic Frontier Foundation, and member of U.S. Vice President Al Gore's National Information Infrastructure Advisory Council. Now she sits on the boards of about a dozen companies from Mountain View, California, to Moscow. And more. Much more. But first and foremost, Esther is a networker and communicator. And her ability to influence the lives of others with her ideas is both unique and impressive. Her newsletter, Release 1.0, has been making and breaking tech companies for nearly two decades. And as chairman of the Internet Corporation for Assigned Names and Numbers (ICANN), she leads an international agency established under the Clinton administration and charged with setting policy for the Internet's core infrastructure, independent of government control.

Esther's intelligence cuts across many disciplines, and her passions make her hard to track down. She travels back and forth so frequently between the U.S. and Eastern Europe—where her EDventure Holdings company hosts an annual technology forum—that she's earned about 400 passport stamps since March 1995. As her Web site reflects [**www.edventure.com**], she's focused on emerging technologies (groupware, artificial intelligence, the Internet, wireless applications), emerging markets (Eastern Europe), and emerging companies. So when we caught up with her, we asked for her take on women's representation in the evolution and application of IT. "Well, I mean, they're not really present. And it's not that things would be so much different with women there. [But] women might be different," she said, from her New York office. "In the last week, I've had countless meetings. Everywhere from London to Tel Aviv. I sat with one woman at lunch. Aside from that, it's all been men."

Lots of women are being left out of the IT equation: not assuming leadership roles in our digital culture; not influencing the development and application of information technology. Why? Esther believes women are not so much being "blocked" as they're being discouraged: "It's subtle. I mean, it doesn't say, 'Women need not apply.' But it's a two-way street. Women need to show up and be a part of things. And it's simply [that] women aren't there."

The early days of cyberspace were dominated by men, but Esther was there. She began using the Net, via MCI Mail, back in 1985, and used a UNIX-to-UNIX copy program even earlier to communicate with Russian programmers she'd met on her first trip to Russia in April 1989. ("I started using email in the pre-Net days in a very, very practical way and the stuff I was using was horrible. Totally obnoxious and hostile to use. Just like they use on airplanes now. I marvel at how they spend millions to come up with such a crummy interface!") Esther insists she's an exception to gender lines demarcating cyberspace or its power paradigms. "I'm an odd person [exclusive of] the gender because I'm not running a corporation, and I didn't rise through a corporate hierarchy." Indeed, she influences by communicating, by registering her unique, virtual voice in the digital world rather than controlling a company or controlling huge amounts of capital. She's a global networker who expresses her ideas via her columns, books, and newsletters, and shapes the flow of business and policy by events she organizes (such as PC Forum and the High-Tech Forum in Europe) and by advising governments about governance of the Net and related matters.

Her job as ICANN chairman is a tough one: it seems ICANN's every move is questioned and, often, attacked. But the corporation also has strong backers: as part of its commitment to spend $100 million (US) advancing the public's voice on digital-age policies, Zoë Baird and the Markle Foundation (see p. 5) committed major monies and gathered nonprofit public interest groups together to help ICANN create a worldwide general membership that will give individuals a say in electing its board members.

Esther's parents played a significant role in shaping this female IT pioneer. Fluent in Russian, she inherited a deep interest in Russia from father Freeman Esther, a renowned astrophysicist who was involved in U.S.–Soviet relations during the Cold War. "My parents gave me scientific curiosity, and my mother was a model of a mother who took it for granted that she'd work in unfeminist fields." Since her parents divorced when she was still quite young, Esther assumed a lot of responsibility at an early age: she regularly traveled by plane on her own between her parents' homes as a youngster, and was "semi-responsible" for younger brother George. ("Who's, actually, pretty wonderful. He recently wrote and published a book [*Darwin Among the Machines: The Evolution of Global Intelligence*], which was far more intellectual than my book [*Release 2.0: A design for living in the digital age*]. His is a very good book about the technical and philosophical underpinnings of the Internet, and he's now working on another one. It's a project my father did when my brother was five, and I was seven: to build a nuclear-powered space ship.")

In an age of mega mergers, Esther's love of the little guy, of small Eastern European software companies and new digital frontiers, has seen some label her a romantic. "I am a romantic . . . but I always was a skeptical romantic about everything. I wanted peace, love, and brotherhood and I studied economics [at Harvard] because I figured that was probably the key to figuring out how the world worked. And if you want to change the world, you have to figure out how it works first." One way to influence and alter the world we live in is the way Esther's doing it: Online.

The Internet gives people power, she says: on the Net, the speaker and the listener are pretty much equal; they're interacting on an equal basis, unlike our one-way, traditional broadcasting mediums. As she sees it, the Net is less a giant library and more a medium about interaction between people; and this ability to connect and communicate, potentially, shifts power.

In an essay (see sidebar, opposite page) written for a special millennium issue of *The New York Times Magazine* focusing on women, Esther looks at women's traditional and common problem with being heard, with assuming power and roles of leadership. She says the Internet is tailor-made to help women finally find their voices. Offline, women are physical entities whose presence and ideas are often—consciously or unconsciously—filtered out, discounted, co-opted. Online, they can express an idea and own it; influence others; have equal access and opportunity for exchange.

The Internet is a medium that may change the balance of power. But first, she says, women have to show up.

"The Sound of the Virtual Voice"
by Esther Dyson

Not long ago, Ann Winblad, a successful venture capitalist well-known on the hi-tech circuit, stood up to speak at a conference. She tapped the microphone and enquired sweetly, "Does this pick up women's voices?" If Ann Winblad, with a sterling track record and millions yet to invest, can ask that, consider what it's like for most women. We now get the mike at conferences in part because organizers are consciously trying to balance things, and in part because many of us simply deserve it—but overall, women still have trouble being heard. Can cyberspace change that? Or will it, like so many other tools and technologies, simply become a way for the old order to reinforce itself? Powerful tools in powerful hands tend to increase the concentration of power, but the Internet isn't just a tool. It's a medium that may change the balance of power.

Consider some history. Long ago, women's work was defined by women's bodies: they bore children and were generally weaker. Gradually, as work became less physical and personal service became a commodity rather than something one did at home, women joined the workforce as nurses, servants, and governesses. As the world industrialized and dexterity began to matter more than strength, they became machine operators. In many semiconductor plants, especially overseas in countries where discrimination is legal, women are still preferred today for their smaller fingers and the precision with which they can work. And as work began to include information, many women became telephone operators, typists, clerks, and secretaries.

Then economic pressures started changing society and social changes began affecting work patterns. As our economy has grown and become ever more competitive, the stock market and other pressures are focusing on performance rather than status, and capable women have begun to get the work they deserve. Increasingly, people are promoted more for performance; businesses can't afford to do otherwise in a competitive market. Women can get good jobs based on performance—at least up to the highest reaches of many companies. I wish that were reliably true. Twenty years ago, we thought that the hi-tech world would by now be different, that women would succeed in large numbers because this was a world where performance counted. It hasn't turned out that way. Women still have a tough time making it into management. We're still socialized to look to men for leadership. Power is based not on performance alone but on presence and personality—and perceptions of personality. In business, women still face a different world from men.

I recall the first board meeting of the Electronic Frontier Foundation I ever attended, way back in 1990 or 1991. I had been invited to join the board by Mitch Kapor, the entrepreneur and developer of Lotus 1-2-3 and an enlightened person if ever there was one. I knew the other board members, who all respected me. But I couldn't get a word in edgewise. Why? I couldn't imagine any reason other than that I spoke with a female voice. It was a shock. These were no traditional troglodytes in suits; they were my kind of people, striving to build a new world on the Net. (At the next meeting we had a female facilitator, and it went a lot better.)

It's a common experience for other women and girls, from second-grade classrooms to boardrooms. And the high-tech industry is really no better than most. I've been to meetings where a woman ventures a comment and is ignored. Minutes later a man makes the same point and is noticed. Now, however, as high-tech products are being integrated into day-to-day business, people are using the Internet not just to order products and retrieve information but also to communicate. They use it to discuss issues, manage teams, negotiate contracts. There's enough Net time for people—women, that is—to establish themselves without a physical presence. In other words, it's the users of the Internet, rather than the sellers of the Internet, that are changing fastest. As a communications medium where personal presence is primarily text and sex differences are not immediately visible, the Internet is tailor-made to help women finally find their voices. And if women feel (rightly or wrongly) stifled in corporate environments, they can more easily strike out for themselves. The information, access, and productivity once available only to big businesses are now accessible to individual entrepreneurs.

Recently, as the interim chairman of the Internet Corporation for Assigned Names and Numbers (ICANN), I have become part of a world full of discussions over so-called mailing lists, where people email their ideas to large groups for comment. It's not a gender-free or character-free world. But gender is less noticeable in our interactions online; what are noticeable are the words on the screen: does this person make sense? When I first started, the names meant nothing; now I have some notion of what to expect from each: insight, whining, skepticism. Yes, people have online personalities, but their sex does not generally color how people read their thoughts. On these networks, women write in the same variety of ways as men.

But you can say your piece and post it without being interrupted midway. The Net enforces a certain fairness by putting everything up on the screen without fear or favor. Yes, there are filtering tools, and there are certain people many people filter out. But that usually has to do with content, not gender.

Online, I'm sure some people may filter me out, but it doesn't happen the way it does off-line—unconsciously. Yes, people may discount what women write, but they are more likely to read it. My online voice does not have a high pitch of the kind that many men find hard, for whatever reason, to hear. Another common experience of women—having your good idea picked up later and attributed to someone else—is less likely to happen on the Web. There's a record, and there are subtle ways of pointing back to it if you are missed.

Net-based discussion is likely to become increasingly important in the way teams of people communicate, in politics, business, or other endeavors. It is important for women to join this online world. But leadership goes beyond discussion to carrying things forward. It requires making decisions that can't be made by consensus; it's about absorbing the uncertainty everyone feels by making a decision and taking responsibility for it. That's still not something most women are trained to do. But I'm hopeful that online experience will help. The Net won't change everything, but it's one more tool to overcome the destiny of biology. The explicit rule is that we're equal, and new habits may make it so. The ability to earn money at work has made a huge difference in the balance of power at home. May the ability to be heard at work now make a huge difference in the balance of power out in the world.

(Originally published in the New York Times on May 16, 1999.)

work

introduction

When I was in university I couldn't possibly have imagined the career I have today. I'd never heard of the Web, had no idea how to operate a computer, and certainly had no idea that it might be possible to build a career in Internet strategy and development. Computers weren't part of my education and no one suggested they should be.

Instead, like many women of my generation, I was encouraged to pursue a traditional and better-understood career path. My girlfriends and I went to school imagining we'd become teachers, lawyers, engineers, or scientists. And some of us did. But thousands of us have instead jumped headfirst into technology careers and are now Web designers, Internet strategists, programmers, video game developers, and network administrators.

The women who have found themselves, as I have, immersed in the uncharted waters of technology are ambitious, hard-working, and out to change the world. They're surviving life at dotcoms, launching their own start-ups, and navigating today's technology corporations. Often working without a precedent, these women have staff photos that look more like frat photos or sometimes have no staff at all. And they're all taking advantage of the opportunities created in an industry that cites a lack of knowledge workers as its greatest obstacle to growth.

Today the information technology sector is growing faster than any other industry. Talented people are in high demand and salaries are high, as a visit to the Career Opportunities section of any technology company's Web site will undoubtedly demonstrate. For many of us, though, the careers we see listed on Web sites are ones we don't understand.

In this section of *Technology With Curves* we'll share stories from women who are out there exploring these workplaces of the future. Their stories of work in the hi-tech sector will shed light on the laundry list of job opportunities you see listed at technology company sites. They remind us that here, like everywhere, the most important skills you can bring to the table include project management, communication, and the ability to work in a fast-paced, team-oriented environment.

The women you'll read about here should, if they don't already, have their own speaking tours. Hearing them talk about starting companies, raising capital, funding companies, writing code, and leading teams is what inspired *Technology With Curves*. These women, who have all at times felt isolated by technology, have now embraced it. More importantly, their careers have benefited from technology and technology has benefited from them.

Looking forward it seems once again impossible to imagine what the job descriptions of the future will be. New technologies will be invented, each one creating career paths for us to explore and presenting unique opportunities for women to play a central role in the industries these groundbreaking women already call home.

Emma Smith

Geraldine Laybourne
"Breathing Life into Broadcasting"

www.oxygen.com

First, Gerry Laybourne teamed up with entertainment
mogul Oprah Winfrey and Hollywood producers Marcy
Carsey, Tom Werner, and Caryn Mandabach to make a new
network for women that converges the Internet and cable
TV. Now, she's trying to make new technology reflect
women's voices. But before all that, Gerry Laybourne was a
smart girl who grew up to be a school teacher. Here is her
history lesson.

Lives and landscapes often evolve simultaneously. Consider
two people, on different sides of the planet. The year is
1955. Today, the landscape is digital, but a half-century ago
life was simpler yet equally complex. Television was in its
infancy. The Space Race had yet to begin. And that year
Russian writer Boris Pasternak completed *Doctor Zhivago*.

BARBARA VAUGHN

Pasternak's epic novel would win
a Nobel Prize, and the Russian
government, which refused to
publish the manuscript, would
pressure him not to accept the
award. But Pasternak celebrates:
his story of the tragic upheavals
in 20th-century Russia is alive;
his novel's characters, with all
their flawed greatness, passions,

and human frailties, are set free on paper.

That same year, an American schoolgirl named Gerry Laybourne sat focused, too, on a piece of paper, hunched at a desk with pen in hand. Her father, stockbroker Paterson Bond, watches as his eight-year-old daughter scratches out homework figures. On his Saturday visits to the office, he brings Gerry along and encourages her to study company portfolios and make investment choices. "My father was amazing, and among other things . . . a great storyteller," she says. Bond is also reputed to have hired the first female stock-broker in New Jersey. "He really believed his daughters could do anything and he saw some-thing in me, yes, but I think he took me along on those trips because he felt sorry for me: I was sandwiched in between a beautiful and perfect older sister, and a charis-matic and brilliant younger sister."

Young Gerry's Saturday-at-the-office investment picks, while often accurate, were rarely followed. Fair enough: after all, who invests in the business advice of eight-year-olds?

Two years later, in 1957, kids like Gerry are pouring over a newly published book called The Cat in the Hat. Doctor Zhivago is published that year too—in Italy. And in the heavens, above the heads of Russian authors headed for exile and American girls headed for school, a metal sphere about the size of a beach ball is launched into Earth's orbit. Sputnik didn't do much by today's high-tech standards: it didn't take photographs or beam images or telephone transmissions home. It just sent out a simple radio signal. But the message was clear: the Soviets had beaten America into space.

The U.S. begins investing heavily in military research, science, and technology, and, by the late 1960s, a young engineer named Paul Baran comes up with a revolutionary idea: a "fishnet-like" communications concept. His idea is this: break messages into fragments, send them via a network of redundant lines, then use a code to reassemble them at their destination. This way, should a portion of the network be destroyed, the "fishnet" system would make U.S. military communications invulnerable in the event of a Soviet nuclear attack. Life, luckily, goes on, and computer pioneers build on Baran's concept, which evolves into a fragmented computer-to-computer communications network: the Internet.

Geraldine Laybourne grows up too. The intelligence her father prized earns her a master's degree in elementary education and a feel for what children's television ought to be. She and her husband Kit, a filmmaker and educator, open a production company and approach a cable network called Nickelodeon with an idea for a TV pilot. Gerry lands a job that leads to a career in innovative programming. Over the next 16 years, she helps take Nickelodeon from a little-known network to a multi-billion-dollar asset by betting on TV shows that don't talk down to children.

Today, as women move online en masse, she's building on that programming experience—which includes an executive run at Disney/ABC Cable Networks—by creating an empire that converges television and the Internet and speaks to women. Oxygen Media Inc. is fueled by big bucks and even bigger talent: $400 million (US) has come from such investment heavyweights as America Online and Microsoft cofounder Paul Allen. Oxygen Media partners Marcy Carsey,

Tom Werner, and Caryn Mandabach (the creators of *The Cosby Show* and *Roseanne*) are programming the new network, and TV talk-show titan Oprah Winfrey completes Oxygen's formidable partnership alliance.

Gerry credits Hollywood TV producer Marcy Carsey with being a catalyst for bringing Winfrey on board. "Marcy knew Oprah slightly better than I did; she runs this very successful independent production company—probably the most successful ever in the history of Hollywood—and runs it her way. They've had hit after hit because she tries to figure out how to serve the audience and not be condescending, and these things are really important to Oprah. For [Oprah], it's more about the principles—and [the] principals involved. The people and the ideas." Some media reports suggested that when the Oxygen Media team approached Winfrey, she immediately embraced the concept of a converged Net–cable TV medium directed at women. "I think it wasn't too immediate . . . Oprah is a very careful person and [her involvement] happened over the course of a couple of months," Gerry recalls. "She was in the middle of a publicity tour for *Beloved*, and her focus was very much on the movie and her involvement in it. Our conversation [with Oprah] centered more on our intention toward women—how we were going to serve them. The Internet-related element of the Oxygen Media vision is, ultimately, what Winfrey subscribed to," she says. "I think Oprah saw that she needed to understand that we were serious students [of the Net] and this would be a good place for her to learn."

What Gerry and her partners are exploring is how the Internet can empower an audience. Digital controls are dynamic; interactivity puts power in the hands of the consumer. Traditional media, such as TV and radio, have always been about taking a piece of creative work and placing it in front of an audience. The audience simply absorbs it. With the Internet—a dynamic versus a static, one-way medium—"it's much more about the audience," she says. And as any regular viewer knows, an empowered audience is what Oprah Winfrey's all about.

As a 25-year-old teacher at Concord Academy, one of America's most elite schools, Gerry Laybourne matured into an educator who valued media as a teaching tool. But educational TV, she says, never really worked because it reflected the hierarchical, Father-Knows-Best, talk-down approach to learning. The Internet, on the other hand, changes the equation and puts the learner/viewer/surfer in the driver's seat. She says the Internet's a great teacher and a great research tool: it lets you know, every day, every minute, what questions women are asking, what they want to know. Gerry says she plans to turn that feedback into television and Web programming. Based on research gathered in focus groups, online, during a cross-country research tour, and in one-on-one interviews, the Oxygen team has learned lessons. Namely, women don't want a hierarchical voice that tells them what to do or think. They want choices. They want different perspectives. They want to draw value from other people's real-life experiences and see if those insights can be applied to their own lives. Women want to be entertained, but they also lead practical, busy lives. "For our audience, we have been particularly concerned about the fact that women have been slower to go on the Web. Women are now about 50 percent of Web users. But if you think about what the Internet enables, it makes sense that women should be 70 percent of the users today. We [women] buy everything. We have to research everything. Our life's work is very complicated."

When the philanthropic Markle Foundation announced in July 1999 that it would spend $100 million (US) on various Internet ventures over the next three to five years, the largest initial award—$4.5 million—went to Oxygen Media. Most of that money was given to a separate business partnership, Oxygen-Markle Pulse. The entity's official aim is to "enhance the influence of the audience over the creation of content" by gathering audience feedback from Oxygen's Web and cable properties and widely distributing that data back to the public. At the time of the announcement, Markle president Zoë Baird (see p. 5) noted in the press that it is the big Internet firms who most need the infusion of foundation money. Why? They're the ones that can reach the masses, said Zoë.

"When Zoë came into the Oxygen world, she had made a big decision. Her aim was to try and come in, at this point in time, when it wasn't too late to bring women in on the ground floor and get their voice heard in the shaping of new technology. And that was exactly the same language that I had been speaking. For us at Oxygen, it's all about cocreation and how we can put more tools in the hands of our audience, so that we can find that voice. And that's just a completely different approach from the way traditional media have thought."

Oxygen's New York City headquarters are housed in three floors of a beautiful, rambling old brick building that used to be a Nabisco cookie factory. In the production area inspired by Gerry's husband—which comes complete with a DJ who spins tunes—Internet producers and television producers share comfortable, open-concept quarters. They jointly fish for issues, stories, and personalities, and stir the content into a converged delivery system, using audience feedback via email and chat-rooms as a constant stimulus and market gauge. The strategy behind Oxygen is to deliver loads and loads of original content.

Gerry believes women want technology that delivers something practical in their lives. From their online feedback, the Oxygen media team has already learned that its audience is fascinated by real stories with real solutions from real women. "We're community building," she says. On the Oxygen Web site, Gerry describes herself as an entrepreneur interested in changing the media landscape. "Having figured out how to change the television landscape for kids in the '80s and '90s, I'm now working to connect women in the 21st century to converged media [TV, computer, and telephone]. And I'm basically a steamroller in front of a talented group of people, making way for them to do their best work."

Mothers make good executives, she says. They have to multitask like mad, and their lives are a finely orchestrated balance of relationships, responsibilities, juggled schedules, and commitments to many people with many needs. Gerry says motherhood was basic training for the business world: from son Sam, once a terrible-two-year-old who's now a high school teacher in Manhattan, she learned how to provide service to an irrational customer; from daughter-turned-actress Emmy, Gerry learned about how to feed a creative side first nurtured by her mother, Gwen. "I had this wonderful package of a father who was a venturous businessman and a great storyteller, and a mother who'd been a radio soap opera writer, producer, and actress. It was just a great combination because she was always doing crazy things, like turning off the television before the end of the show and making us write the ending."

Her children, like her parents, certainly influenced Gerry's professional progress. "I think I've been following [Sam and Emmy] around for my whole life. The first thing I did when we launched Oxygen was to sit down with them, and they just talked about what their views of this digital world were. Sam, who teaches English, actually uses the Web to motivate his kids, and ironically does a lot of the same kind of media education that his father and I did when we were teachers." Gerry pioneered kids' television programming by—like her father before her—listening to children. Now she's listening, in an intimate and an interactive way, to women. In the process, she and her Oxygen Media partners may change the way women think about the Web, about television, and about the converged value these media have in our lives. Age-old questions resonate across the centuries, across lines of gender and time: can I gain insights into my life from looking at someone else's? How do another person's flaws and strengths and experiences relate to my own?

Characters in epic novels like *Dr. Zhivago* and *Anna Karenina* wrestled with these questions—the big questions and the small worries that make up everyone's life. Today, when we want to look at real life, we often skip the classic novels and, instead, turn to mediums that create windows into real lives. A new digital window is being opened for women and families. At Oxygen Media, Gerry's team wants to converge the Web and TV into a medium that's a breath of fresh air for women. What will women and their families want from new converged media, like the Oxygen network? Likely it will be a mixture of the simple and the profound, life being what it is. Almost certainly, voices and stories—captured by technology and set free in the imaginations of an audience—will shape our digital world. What Boris Pasternak could not conceive of in his wildest Russian dreams is now a seed of thought in the mind of a young girl or boy in the new millennium. Stay tuned.

Gerry Laybourne picks a powerful partner:
Oprah Winfrey

What kind of impact can Oprah have online? Consider the marketing tidal wave that two words—"Oprah's Picks"—created in the book publishing industry. Now consider the impact that sort of connecting power could have on a growing audience as morphable, impressionable, and downright fickle as the one seeking the Internet.

Women not only watch Oprah, they listen to her. As women flood online, Oprah could create some powerful currents with her personal directives. Certainly, the audience is there. Less than two weeks before Oxygen Media launched its new cable TV channel on February 2, 2000, news wires carried stories and surveys announcing that the Internet gender gap had officially closed: the rate at which women were climbing online was officially outpacing that of men. The studies also drew gender lines defining online behavior: men seem to prefer news, business, and information sites, while the majority of women seek health and lifestyle information.

When the most powerful woman in television ventured online for the first time, she took her millions of audience members with her. Guided by their own Internet guru, Oprah and her best friend took a 12-part course on the online world; they explored everything from email to chats to search engines to home pages, and reported their impressions on how the Web will change the way women look at money, shopping, education, and technology. (The series, entitled "Oprah Goes Online," is among the partnerships and initiatives praised by the U.S. government on their new Digital Divide Web site [**www.digitaldivide.gov/**], dedicated to closing the gap between technology's haves and have-nots. See sidebar: The Digital Divide, p. 13.)

Oprah's ability to bond with her audience sets her

apart. She not only shares information with her audience, she connects. And what she says influences the decisions people make. The day after a guest on her program declared that hamburgers could be hazardous to one's health, cattle futures dropped 11 percent. When the cattlemen sued her shortly thereafter, Oprah took her show onto their turf and delivered her program from the Texas panhandle. The cattlemen battled Oprah in the courts. But even as they fought their unsuccessful fight, their wives fought for tickets to see her show.

Something else to consider: Oprah delivers. Early in her television career, she revealed she'd been molested by a cousin and an uncle. Years later—when she had the power of professional success behind her—she hired a law firm to work on drafting a bill to submit to Congress for the purpose of establishing an American precedent: a national registry of sex offenders. The bill was signed by President Clinton and became law in 1994.

One woman. One life. And now, she's online.

Kim Polese
"Brewing JAVA, Building Business"

www.marimba.com

Kim Polese is one of the leading women in technology. Kim helped to create the computer language, JAVA, while at Sun Microsystems. Now she heads up her own software company in California. Kim says if she's one of the few women out front in the high-tech world her parents are to blame: they encouraged her to embrace science and technology at a very early age, and to explore her potential with a child's sense of abandon.

As one of the few female chief executives in Silicon Valley, Kim Polese knows the importance of building her own network. The cofounder of Marimba, Inc., a company that develops software solutions, had already proven herself as a talented computer programmer, but when she found herself at the helm of a high-tech firm in the midst of a male-

dominated industry, she knew just what to do.

Kim kick-started a monthly dinner meeting ritual for a sampling of female senior executives from various Valley-based technology and investment companies. Dubbing themselves "Babes in Boyland," the women are tongue-in-cheek about the name, but serious about the purpose of their female-only get-togethers. Kim explains, "We really get a lot out of meeting with each other. And it isn't about sharing war stories of being women in this industry. It's about, 'Hey, I am looking for a really great VP of engineering. Do you know of any recruiters?' or 'How did you manage moving your licensing model from perpetual to subscription?' I mean, real issues, having to do with running companies."

These like-minded businesswomen have sought each other out in an effort to share insights and information over a great meal, but many of them, including Kim, also have firsthand experience with the backlash of being a "babe in boyland." In her late thirties, Kim knows what it's like to have her youth and appearance used against her in attempts to undermine her stellar success with Marimba. "I have discovered that any time there is something new or different, it creates controversy. It's new, or unusual, anyway, to have a young woman as a CEO of a high-visibility technology company. And that, unfortunately, is the fact today and it may be for some time to come—and any time there is something unusual it instantly attracts critics."

Kim has decided to take this criticism in stride and recognize it as how the human psyche works and, in particular, how the press works. "One of the things the press really loves to do is create controversy and drama. And you can't do that without setting up the winners and the losers, or focusing on a company's upswing and then the fall from grace." Despite Marimba's successful debut and a 1999 initial public offering that catapulted the firm's market value as high as $1.4 billion (US), there are those who want to profile Marimba as a company caught in a repeat comeback cycle; that is, building the company up as a success story only to tear it down again. Kim tries to remain amused at this media tactic because she is confident of her own version of reality, which reveals that Marimba has never stumbled and has only strengthened as a market leader since 1996.

Nevertheless, Kim is not so amused by the media's tendency to focus on the appearance of female executives rather than their leadership capability. "When a female CEO of a company is profiled by the press, the lead comment in many articles is about her appearance. It is so unfortunate that this aspect is considered to be a normal part of a woman executive's capabilities, or characteristics, in a way that [it] never is for a man. This is getting worse rather than better. It really goes to the emphasis society still places on how a woman looks, and how important that is. And the advertising messages around us that are given to young girls growing up has really been limiting and damaging on many levels."

Despite these societal challenges, Kim is one "babe in boyland" who definitely likes to take the focus off herself and put it squarely back on her company and her team. "What I like most about my job is working together with a team of really smart people to build groundbreaking technology solutions that make companies successful. I love being able to go to a Home Depot, or a Schwabb, and help them to capitalize on the power of the Internet to connect with their customers, and know that we are making a major difference in that company's ability to succeed in this new Internet age. But the most fun is doing that together with a team. I love working with people who are driven by really cool technology. Not just technology itself, but making sure that it applies to solving real problems in the world today."

As CEO of a growing company with 200 employees, Kim's leadership style is based on an open-door policy. For example, the "lunch with Kim" monthly ritual invites six to eight employees to join her for a meal at a local restaurant, and regular "Executive Roundtable" meetings enable staff to

Ada Byron Lovelace

Imagine having a computer language named after you! The U.S. Department of Defense computer language, ADA, recognizes Ada Byron Lovelace's contribution to the development of the computer. Ada, daughter of the poet Lord Byron, collaborated with Charles Babbage in the 1840s on the analytical engine, the forerunner of the modern computer. In 1843, Ada wrote a scientific paper that anticipated the development of computer software (including the term "software"), artificial intelligence, and computer music.

Annie Wood

Inventive Women

www.inventivewomen.com

meet with the entire executive staff to discuss whatever is on their minds. Marimba also holds monthly "All Hands" meetings where all employees gather to discuss company challenges and future strategy. By actively encouraging and listening to her staff, Kim hopes to guarantee her firm's high retention rate and ensure her employees remain an integral part of a motivated team.

Formerly a key member of Sun Microsystem's software development crew, Kim certainly knows the value of winning teamwork. As the cofounder of JAVA, the programming language that has since revolutionized the technology industry, she cites her time at Sun as a watershed in her computer career. Once a girl whose only goal was to win her school science fair, Kim had no idea she would one day become a computer scientist and eventually have a hand in determining the world's high-tech future.

The daughter of Italian immigrant parents, Kim was encouraged to take advantage of all the intriguing opportunities that America had to offer, especially in the emerging field of technology. At a young age Kim began to explore the science realm, and on a school trip to the Lawrence Hall of Science in California, she discovered "Eliza"—a computer program designed as a virtual psychiatrist who could have "conversations" with users. "I would go back and spend hours and hours trying to trip her up, to get her to say something repetitive to prove she was just a computer." Kim later learned that Eliza was one of the first artificial intelligence programs ever written, and credits her experience with Eliza for being the catalyst that turned her on to science. The rest, as they say, is "herstory," as Kim went on to study biophysics at Berkeley and computer science at the University of Washington, and forged a path as a software pioneer, entrepreneur, and role model for young women around the world.

As one of the few female leaders in the industry, Kim takes her responsibility very seriously. "If I can be an inspiration . . . if I can make some young girl in junior high school think, *Wow, technology is really cool because you can start companies and run them, just like Kim has,* then I feel like I've succeeded in a very, very important way. And just as important as building a great company, is making sure that all of society is really benefiting from this technology success that we are creating here."

Determined to bridge the "digital divide" and to encourage young women to become future architects of technology, Kim is on a mission to prove that "technology is fun and the field is not just about making money; it's about creation and it's about innovation." Kim still claims that at age 38 she hasn't lost her childhood zest for technology, and she still gets really "jazzed" about the new products that Marimba is building and the new ways to solve hard problems, technically, for her customers.

The expanding field of high-tech architecture is another pet source of enthusiasm, and Kim is thrilled by the emerging opportunities to combine art with technology. In a recent interview, Kim speculated that there will soon "be a whole generation of da Vincis in software development—

that is, those who can envision patterns and architectures and the way the networks work together." Kim believes this brilliant new breed will understand how these systems work and have the ability to use them in a way that stretches beyond our current collective imagination. "There's a creative aspect to software development that I think people aren't aware of. In fact, in our own company there are software developers who are also musicians and artists because it is spatial reasoning, it's patterns, fluidity. There is a lot more to it than just cranking out code."

According to Kim, these "digital da Vincis" will be valued tremendously, and they'll be at the heart of many great companies to be built in the years to come.

This positive portrayal of the future is a far cry from the current high-tech reality, wherein an entire generation of young people seem determined to forgo creativity in favor of benefiting from easy money. "What makes Silicon Valley great are things like creativity and innovative thinking and building great companies for the long term. What is happening today is people are forgetting those basics, and the concept of building a company for the long term is almost an afterthought. And I find that very disturbing, because I think that can create problems that ultimately undermine the ability of Silicon Valley to continue to succeed."

As a young but relatively seasoned CEO, Kim is troubled by the gold-rush mentality of the myriad youth minting small fortunes in the Valley. "I have a sense of responsibility about it too, because I do feel that, especially as young leaders here in this industry, we have a choice. We can either focus on the greed or cash-out factor, or we can take the larger view here and say, 'Let's build companies for the long term. Let's make our customers successful. Let's make our investors successful for the long term. Let's make those our values that we have as our core. And also, let's make sure we are doing everything we can to spread the influence and the wealth of this technology boom that we are creating to all members of society, not just to the privileged few here in the Valley.'"

Determined to resist the short turnaround temptation, Kim is in favor of building a durable company based on a strong set of ethics and effective leadership. Instead of a money-grabbing mindset, the Marimba mission is "to build a company for the long term; that is something that is a core value, and it doesn't matter what the stock is doing today or tomorrow, it matters what it is doing a year from now, or two years from now. And that is what we need to be focused on at all times."

What recommendation does Kim offer the next tech-savvy generation eager to join the current dotcom frenzy? "To younger people who don't understand the basic values of building companies, I would say, 'This is serious. This is not a game. This is not about me, me, me or cashing out. This is about constructing great companies.'"

Setting an example as a business architect, Kim is building her own company to last, and she feels excited and privileged to be leading Marimba in the new millennium. "This is a critical time for high-tech, and I believe that we have an awesome responsibility to get it right and to make a difference." Despite being a pioneer in a competitive, fast-paced, and oft-times greedy industry, Kim knows what's important. "It's the network. Nothing else is predictable, and in order to succeed you have to build a loyal team and create a network of trusted people." Sound advice from one smart "babe in boyland."

Sarah Flannery
Cryptographer

In January 1999, international news wires carried the story of a 16-year-old Irish teenager named Sarah Flannery. A student in County Cork, they said she had devised a code for sending secret messages by computer at record-breaking speed. Sarah Flannery had used the science of cryptography to design a code—a data-encryption technology considered to be potentially better than the battle-tested encryption algorithm of RSA Data Security Inc., used to convert confidential information so that it could travel the Internet and be sent via email.

Sarah got the idea for the algorithm during a weeklong work-experience program at the Dublin, Ireland–based data-security company Baltimore Technologies. The idea, she said, was to exploit "non-commutativity of matrix multiplication, and avoid a step which slows the RSA algorithm." U.S. encryption experts viewed the pronouncement of equal

security with some skepticism; for any encryption to be taken seriously, they said, it takes years of analysis and review; but media reports flashed around the world with news about Sarah's work.

Soon Ireland's newest media star was receiving job offers from international computer companies. Judges described her work as "brilliant"; in fact, one judge advised her to patent it. But the young cryptographer said she'd rather publish her findings than patent them. "What a storm in a teacup that created," recalls Sarah's father, David, who lectures mathematics at Cork Institute of Technology. Indeed. The media couldn't believe it: in this age of dotcom billionaires and initial public offerings, here was someone who didn't want to make a fast fortune on a digital discovery.

Sarah's project was mainly about maths: she'd used matrices to formulate an alternative to RSA, the current data protection code devised by three students at the Massachusetts Institute of Technology in 1977. The result: an algorithm, a mathematical blueprint, that was far faster than the RSA. With other systems—including RSA—available at no cost on the Internet, she couldn't see that anyone would pay for her system, even though encryption is vital to financial and business transactions on the Internet. She could patent her discovery, but patenting maths "doesn't help anyone to move science on," she told reporters at the time.

The eldest of five children, Sarah had to go through "lots of stuff" before she finalized her theory. "I reached critical points where I would get stuck for three weeks or so. I just kept thinking about it, and then the whole thing slipped into place."

When she was finished, she named her new code the Cayley-Purser (after Arthur Cayley, an eminent nineteenth-century Cambridge mathematician, and Michael Purser, a cryptographer who inspired and supported her.) Awarded the Intel Excellence Award, she represented Ireland at the International Science and Engineering Fair where she won the Intel Fellows Achievement Award and other honors. Sarah went on to be named The Irish Young Scientist of the Year in 1999.

Mathematicians at the University of Cambridge offer this explanation of Flannery's work on their Millennium Mathematics Project site: "Where RSA uses exponentiation to encode and decode a message, Cayley-Purser uses matrix multiplication. This means that while RSA grows as a cubic with the length of the encryption 'key,' Cayley-Purser grows quadratically. For a typical key length of 1,024 bits, this makes Cayley-Purser around 75 times faster."

Father and daughter reported that the Cayley-Purser has proved, in fact, to have some "security holes," but that does not overshadow one young woman's inspiring work and contribution as a new-generation cryptographer. Bruce Schneier, founder and chief technical officer of Counterpane Internet Security, Inc., greeted reports of security holes with this assessment in the industry publication *CryptoGram*'s December 1999 issue: "Flannery's paper, describing the Cayley-Purser algorithm, has been published on the Internet by an unknown source. It's interesting work, but it's not secure. Flannery herself publishes a break of the algorithm in an appendix. To me, this makes Flannery even more impressive as a young cryptographer. As I have said many times before, anyone can invent a new cryptosystem. Very few people are smart enough to be able to break them." Flannery, with her father's help, has just published a book called *In Code: A Mathematical Journey*, published by Profile Books of London, England.

Jeannine Parker

President & CIO (Chief Innovation Officer)
Jparker Company
www.jparker.com

Jeannine Parker says she "fell in love with computers in '85 and wound up marrying her Macintosh in '86." Since then, Jeannine (aka JP) has flirted with interactive innovations from CD-ROM development to database design, and today is immersed in another intimate relationship—this time, with the Internet. You might say this entrepreneur is now "wedded to the Web," and she claims that it was love at first sight: "When I first saw hypertext on the Net, I glimpsed the future intuitively. I knew immediately that it was only a matter of time before someone would write a GUI for the World Wide Web, and the broadband world we're talking about today would come hurtling toward us."

Long before e-commerce and dotcoms, Jeannine, 36, was well known for growing innovative Internet companies.

Today, she is president and chief innovation officer of her own company, Jparker Company, a Santa Monica–based strategic positioning firm and think tank for Internet, convergence, and transmedia ventures.

As an Internet advisor, Jeannine helps her clients build sound, sustainable business strategies, then connects them with the creative, technical, and financial resources they need to do it right the first time. She also advises senior executive management in developing and refining their strategic vision, market focus, and positioning, and in negotiating win-win partnerships and deal structures.

Like many women who became entrepreneurs within the high-tech field, Jeannine's business focuses on content and services. As quoted in a recent *Los Angeles Times* article, Jeannine says, "Success of newer companies depends on technological advancements, [and] also good customer relationships, management, and communication, areas in which women traditionally excel."

Jeannine also cites a growing trend of women who opt out of the confines of corporate life to create their own technology ventures. She thinks many are looking for the ownership, control, and flexibility that they can't seem to find in mainstream business. However, she warns that those women who decide to work for large IT companies may face similar barriers to those in traditional business careers. "There's a conceit in the technology industry that we don't care if you're black, male, Martian, or what you're doing . . . unless you happen to be a woman, that is. I call it the Plexiglas ceiling—it flexes, so you actually move, but it's still a ceiling."

Jeannine attributes her own hi-tech breakthrough to the support she received from networking associations. Access to these communities helped pave her way onto the information highway and allowed her to "progress from tech novice to reasonable expertise in a single year."

Thanks to the International Interactive Communications Society (IICS)—and especially to the community she and a small group of her peers built in Los Angeles in 1992 and 1993—Jeannine was thrown into the alphabet soup of new media (from ISP to GUI and everything in between), as well as into the mysteries of the pre-Web Internet. "I had a series of epiphanies about the future, and I was on fire. I taught and wrote and spoke a great deal, and produced a number of conferences about interactive media. At the time I was the crazy one whose panels were titled things like New Media Meets the Net, where I tried—in vain, I might add—to get multimedia developers interested in the Internet. 'Hey, guys,' I said to them, 'c'mon over here! CD-ROM–based multimedia is a transitional moment. The Web's the thing, and you, who really know about navigation and UI and building compelling user experiences, you could *own* this.'

A **GUI** (or Graphical User Interface) is a non command line based interface that uses associative visual representations for applications, files and functions to make navigation more user friendly.

  Microsoft Windows is an example of a G U I; however, the G U I was first developed by Xerox in the 1970s. Apple then applied the idea to the Macintosh and Microsoft brought it to the PC.

Lisa Erbe

Head of Internet Strategy

www.switch-on.co.uk

They glared at me, they didn't want to hear it. They were very protective of their 'edutainment' market, which admittedly had been hard-won."

In 1994, Jeannine helped produce the first public hands-on demonstration of the Web at a new-media trade show. ("It may in fact have been the first one at any trade show.") She had six Macs and six PCs and an ISDN connection, and despite the fact that there was barely any content out there yet ("We demoed Mosaic with The Asylum, Megadeth Arizona, and Kaleidospace, and showed people how to do email"), hers was the most popular exhibit at the show, with lines five people deep, waiting to get in and surf. It was at that time that she left the entertainment field for good and hung out her shingle as an Internet strategist and cultivator of companies. "I haven't looked back. People thought I was nuts, of course, but I was merely a pioneer (see these arrows in my back?)."

Today, Jeannine takes her role as a technology visionary seriously, and she attributes her current hi-tech consultant position to her basic intuition and common sense. "I have a knack for the big picture, for where and how far ideas go, as well as for what will work and what won't. Head in the clouds, but feet on the ground, I guess. That is what led me to where I am today." She says she can always be found at that intersection where artists, technologists, and business-people are having a very spirited discussion about the shape of the future. But she'll never forget that fateful summer in 1985, when she first fell in love with a machine—just a girl and her Apple IIe.

Evany Thomas
Managing Editor
Webmonkey.com

Though I'm now neck-deep in the world of technology, I've never managed to become the kind of "acronympho" this industry is famous for ("We need PHP and XML with a Tcl/Tk SQL backend ASAP"). But I have noticed tech slowly creeping into my language over the years, especially at work. We'll be sitting in a meeting room, sipping double-talls and throwing ideas up on the white board, and I'll actually hear myself utter gems like "Let's take this off-line" (translation: things have become too specific for this general gathering, thus key players should gather at a smaller meeting); "Why don't you view source on that" (find out what it'll take to achieve a particular goal); "Let's bookmark that for later" (address the issue at another time); "I think we've got too many windows open" (the meeting has disintegrated into a cacophony of sub-conversations); and "Let's add that to shopping cart" (what a fabulous idea!).

My all-time favorite kind of techno-speak is terminology born from other slang. The word *extranet* is a perfect example of what can come of this kind of linguistic inbreeding. The term comes from *intranet*,

which refers to a network with a firewall to keep the public at bay—schools and businesses use these. Since *extranet* sounds like the exact opposite of *intranet*, you'd think it would refer to a network open to everyone. But, no! That's the *intERnet*. An *extranet* is actually just a password-protected Web site that gives a user access only to user-tailored sections of the site.

Some other cherished spin-off terminology includes *narrowcast*, which refers to online content sent to a specific group of individuals (versus a *broadcast*, which is available to anyone); *soft copy* (*hard copy* is the printout of a file, so *soft copy* is the electronic version), and a *shutdown* (a failed start-up company).

What's truly amazing is how fast the language of technology spreads from the confines of cubicles to the rest of the world. My family used to have no idea what I did for a living—they just had no frame of reference. But now I go to Thanksgiving dinner and everyone's feverishly pitching *B2B* (that's business to business) Web sites and bragging about eBay coups, while the turkey cools on their plates.

And I find myself wishing that everyone would just dot-calm down already.

Andrea Donnelly

Senior Motion Capture Shoot Supervisor
Mainframe Entertainment Inc.
www.mainframe.ca

We'd probably all like to have a bit more Andrea Donnelly in us. Soft-spoken and self-aware, Andrea has a quiet charm that makes you want to invite her over for dinner and go sky-diving with her at the same time.

For the past three years Andrea has been working for Electronic Arts™ (EA), a leading interactive entertainment software company with offices around the world. EA develops, publishes, and distributes games for personal computers and entertainment systems such as the PlayStation™ and Nintendo® 64. Andrea was hired to be EA's first female motion capture specialist, and hasn't looked back since.

When she found out Electronic Arts had offered her a position in its motion capture department, Andrea was ecstatic. She'd just returned from London, where she'd been

working in a Web café, and was itching to find a way to work in an environment where she could always be learning. Electronic Arts was renowned as the company with the biggest "toy box" around, so this job offer was a dream come true. She couldn't wait to get started.

Andrea was new to almost everything about the video-game

Motion Capture is the name given to using technology to capture movements and then translate those movements onto computerized characters. Motion Capture technology (called MoCap by people "in the know") is used in video games, but also has an array of interesting applications in fields such as medicine, biomechanics, and visual effects.

business and jumped into a trial-by-fire environment less than three hours after arriving for her first day at work. Day 1 at EA was scary, busy, and absolutely nothing like any other job Andrea could have imagined. She hardly even had time to process what she was doing. Within just a few hours of arriving at the office, she was sent to a shoot with the team who was working on NBA '98.

When she arrived at the studio, famous basketball players were wandering around getting ready for their shoot and waiting to be connected to the motion capture equipment that would record their movements for the game. Talk about a one-of-a-kind first day on the job. Andrea quickly found herself being put to work capturing data from the players and entering this data into a database. She learned how to do trigger starts and stops, and so, right away, she was learning—just as she'd hoped.

Andrea continued to rise through the ranks, and eventually became a motion capture specialist who often took management and leadership positions on projects. During preproduction, she acted as the main liaison between the motion capture team and the game team. She generated movement lists and worked with her team to scout out talent, practice with stunt people, and learn from technical advisors.

In the production stage, Andrea moved into a more supervisory role, leading the team through the necessary steps as they actually created and captured the movements they'd so carefully choreographed. But it's in postproduction that she and her team really have their work cut out for them. Here the team members are creating "skeletons" of the bodies whose motions they've captured. They import motion data (which is essentially a bunch of three-dimensional points in space) and map that data onto their skeletons. Throughout the process, Andrea also takes on roles including software evaluation and team training.

The Electronic Arts offices are a 20-something's paradise, complete with basketball courts, game rooms, cafés—and Frisbee competitions at lunchtime. There are other perks to this hi-tech career as well. Since joining EA, Andrea has had the opportunity to appear on television and give interviews in which she's talked about the exciting nature of her work in digital media production. She works hard, but is rewarded for her efforts and feels there are lots of opportunities for her to keep expanding her horizons.

Andrea has had an important impact on her work environment at EA. She's convinced the cafeteria to stock vegetarian dishes, and, after she joined the motion capture team, the studio implemented a new policy stating that only women will "marker up" women who are being modeled for a game, and only men will "marker up" men. Up to that point, there hadn't been any women involved in production and the policy had seemed unnecessary, especially because most of the sports games EA develops feature male athletes rather than female athletes. This is changing now as well.

But being the first woman to join a technology team— although a wonderful experience—hasn't been without its obstacles. Andrea admits to having changed her own behavior since joining EA. She knows that she'd feel awkward wearing a skirt to work and so sticks with casual pants that come in especially handy when she's putting in overtime and wanting to stay as comfortable as possible. Andrea also decided to curtail her femininity in other ways, not because she was trying to be a man, but because she is conscious of how she wants to be perceived and doesn't want her womanhood to be a focus at work.

Andrea works hard to ensure that she is respected at work and also that other women are given the respect and credit they deserve. It wasn't until she joined EA that she realized just how important it was to her that she (and all women) be viewed as smart and capable and skilled. She doesn't date co-workers, sticking with this hard-and-fast rule because being taken seriously and being thought of as a part of the team is a number-one priority for this determined and ambitious motion capture diva.

Not long ago Andrea accepted a position as motion capture supervisor for *Action Man*, a television series being produced by Mainframe Entertainment, and was quickly promoted to senior motion capture shoot supervisor. While she misses life at Electronic Arts, she is excited about this new challenge: trying her hand at motion capture for television.

Tracy Smee

Internet Freedom Fighter
Zero-Knowledge Systems
www.zeroknowledge.com

Tracy Smee is on a mission to defend our rights and protect us from crime. No, she's not a lawyer or a police officer— she's an employee at a software company called Zero-Knowledge Systems. The Montreal-based start-up believes Internet users need to be informed of possible threats to their online privacy as well as other potential pitfalls such as cybercrime. The company also intends to give us Freedom; that is, the encryption software they are developing that they say will give us fail-safe security on the Net.

As content producer and editorial director at Zero-Knowledge, Tracy is currently building a large resource center devoted to educating "Netizens" about their cyber rights. She writes and edits content for the company's Web properties, helps with Web project brainstorming, and develops

Web marketing strategies and concepts. Tracy adds that it's her job to educate people about threats to privacy, and to communicate the unique ability of their product, Freedom, to respond in an empowering way to these threats. To that end, Tracy believes the potential impact that her company, and their product, could have on the

Cookies are commands initiated by the site (or server) and accepted by the client (or browser). Cookies return text from the browser to the site so that, for example, the list of selections in a 'shopping cart' can be associated with a particular user. A cookie can be used to store browser preferences, or even to make the Web less annoying by assuring that no site sends the same advertisement to the browser twice.

future of privacy, the Internet, and even society at large is substantial. She says, "Being part of a solution that will guarantee free speech online, and allow Netizens to live online without annoyance, harassment, or discrimination from any individual, or group or government, is very exciting. It really feels like I'm part of a revolution—Zero-Knowledge employees are called 'Internet Freedom Fighters' for a reason! I couldn't work these insane hours if it were for some faceless shareholder's benefit."

With a strong social purpose to motivate her, Tracy doesn't seem to mind the fast pace of her chosen career: "Our company moves pretty quickly, and people who slow us down tend not to last too long. As the first editorial person on board (not including our super-stars in documentation), I've been lucky enough to have played a part in creating the company's marketing and communications goals, making sure everyone's on the same page in terms of messages, tone, and style. I'm working with people who are jacked about what they are doing, and there's no lack of positive impact here."

She's also attracted to the relaxed environment and atti-tude that we've come to associate with funky new-media firms. "I love our casual atmosphere and our 'anti-dress' code. It's always fun when a consultant comes to work for us for a few weeks. Inevitably there's a progression from suit-and-tie, to sweater-and-tie, to dress-shirt-and-sweater, to polo-shirt-and-slacks, and then various forays into casual-

Fridayness, until they break down and finally start arriving in T-shirt and jeans."

She does have a problem, however, with the dearth of female colleagues in her line of work. "Our company is doing extremely advanced work in cryptography, security, and networks, and has managed to recruit some of the top tech people in the world. So far, all are men. In typical geek fashion, many of them are a little less developed in the social-skill side of things. The fact that I'm a woman certainly doesn't make for the most naturally flowing conversation with this crowd after our 4:30 p.m. Friday beer-and-chip gatherings."

> **Privacy** requires security because, without the ability to control access and distribution of information, privacy cannot be protected. But privacy is not security. Information is secure if the *owner* of information can control that information. Information is private if the *subject* of information can control that information.
>
> L. Jean Camp, PhD
> Assistant Professor
> Harvard University
> Author, *Trust and Risk in Internet Commerce*

Despite the fact that few women are working in her field, at age 30, Tracy has already had a lucrative career in IT. Like most other multimedia people she knows, nothing she studied in school has much to do with her current career, although she claims her education turned out to be a pretty good foundation. "I went to McGill University and graduated with a BA in geography and a minor in environmental studies. I focused on Geographic Information Systems [GIS], a branch of spatial analysis software that uses digital maps and satellite images to learn new things about landscapes. It meant I spent a lot of time in front of a computer."

Her first actual job in technology was working part time as a supervisor in a student computer lab. "I remember the ultra-geeky math students used to come in and hover around one of the 286s with this little blue box labeled 'Gandalf' attached to it. I had no idea what they were doing, but I figured 'Gandalf' had to do with Dungeons and Dragons, so I let them be. Turned out I wasn't too far from the truth—they were using the box to dial in to a BBS to play role-playing games. I completely missed the birth of the Internet, and didn't get involved again until well after it had started to look more like the Internet of today."

Tracy's introduction to computers goes way back. "In the early eighties, my dad brought home a big beige box with a screen in it and introduced me to the 'Superbrain.' I kid you not, it was actually labeled that way, even though I'm sure it was less advanced than a Commodore 64. I used to spend hours in front of it playing a text-based adventure game that ran off a floppy. Computers never intimidated me. I used to take programming day-camp in the summer, but never did anything with it. Writing code just seemed way too boring."

When Tracy was in high school she never imagined she'd have the job she has now. "Not by a long shot. I had absolutely no attraction to journalism when I was in high school, but loved creative writing and poetry and music. I liked computers and electronics, but had no aspirations to be a programmer. I was more interested in figuring out how they worked and messing around with the graphics and the games. Who knew then that I'd be able to put the two together?"

Tracy has always had a capable comfort level with computers, but some aspects of technology definitely frighten her. "I know that what you say and write online can live forever in some database and come back to bite you in the ass when you're trying to get a mortgage or insurance or something. So I don't take chances when I'm online—not until our software comes out! My biggest fear is that technology is concentrating power in the hands of those who wish to control access to information and free expression."

In response, Tracy intends to take back that power and put it in the hands of the people, by continuing to work at her do-gooder day job as well as pursuing justice in her dreams. Her future fantasy is to be a superhero seeking out suppressors of free speech online.

Tracy Smee aka Internet Freedom Fighter.

Amy Kovarick

Agent Provocateur

"Agent provocateur" may sound somewhat like the title of a sexy undercover character in a spy novel, but Amy Kovarick's own definition is "one who challenges. Inspires. Takes risks . . . and unlocks potential."

At 34, Amy is living up to her chosen new-media title and she has the credentials to prove it. Her 12-year career has spanned all aspects of the digital media and Internet business, including strategic planning, sales, new-media production, finance, human resources, and operations. She continues to reinvent herself within the industry.

Amy, an American, arrived in Canada in 1992 and cofounded what has become one of the hottest new-media companies in North America. The company, formerly known as Digital Renaissance (DR), is now called Extend Media, and has become a leading developer of media convergence technologies. Over a period of seven years,

Amy helped nurture the company from 3 to 150 people and a $100-million (US) private valuation. But this multimedia success story began several years earlier with a dream and considerable courage.

In 1987, Amy had been developing CD-ROMs for a U.S. defence contractor in Washington, and at the same time she was having a long-distance relationship with a Canadian. Eventually the pair decided to move to Toronto and build a multimedia company from the ground up. Amy claims she came to Canada "for the guy, the job, and the vision." The relationship didn't last, but the company grew to be a key player in the industry, and Amy established herself as a multimedia maverick.

Amy left DR in 1999 and moved on to other exciting entrepreneurial endeavors, including a brief stint as owner and managing partner of another fledgling new-media company called the NRG Group. Featured in the progressive magazine *Fast Company*, this innovative youth-focused company develops and provides educational programs, performs youth market research, takes on Internet production projects, and nurtures youth-based Internet business start-ups. The company strives to give youth a voice so that they may take their place as leaders of the technological revolution. While at the NRG Group, Amy also toured as a motivational speaker to audiences that ranged from grade seven students to senior executives.

Amy's innovative career path soon established her as a role model for young women in particular, and she continues to strive to encourage young women to embrace technology and the unique career opportunities within the industry. "Young women can usually identify and relate to women more easily than some guys. When I have gone out and spoken to high school classes and at career fairs, I can see it in their eyes. They start off bored, and then you see them getting hooked on your excitement and enthusiasm. They lean forward, their hands dart up in the air with questions, they start to sparkle. Catching them young is the key—lighting the fire as early as possible—believing in the possibilities and their limitless potential. It was long after university that I began to recognize my own potential. If I could have kindled that at a younger age, who knows what more I could have achieved."

On the speaking circuit, Amy was also expected to share her personal recipe for becoming a successful "agent provocateur" within the growing and highly competitive tech-world. Surprisingly, Amy's own cool career was launched courtesy of the U.S. Air Force, when she received a full scholarship for a computer science degree at Lehigh University in Pennsylvania, a private engineering-focused university. "I didn't have a burning passion for technology, but I picked computer science because everyone said computers were a smart thing to do." Amy didn't immediately heed the call of computer geekdom: "The overall concepts and programming itself did intrigue me because of how orderly and rule-based it was. I dig that. However, early on I rebelled against the long hours in the computer lab that seemed to go with the field—there had to be more to life! Frankly, I wasn't an elegant programmer. I didn't get wrapped up in making my code smart and concise. I wasn't fascinated by working out the problems. I just wanted to get it done and keep going. It was the broader concepts and implications of technology that interested me."

Upon graduating, Amy joined the U.S. Air Force Reserves, as required by her scholarship, and took a job as a systems analyst for the Pentagon. Amy assumed she was destined for a computer career in the Air Force until fate provided an opportunity for her to opt out of her obligation, and she was finally free to flee to Canada and fast-forward into her future.   ·

After 12 years of incredible experiences and challenges in new media, Amy decided to take time out and unlock her own potential. "I wanted to learn how to really listen to myself. So, I got in my car and traveled across America. For the first time in my life, I threw away my compulsive need for an agenda and a plan and just drove for five weeks, experiencing whatever felt right and good. I read many spiritual and self-awareness books, thought, wrote, listened, and went deep into myself."

Landing in California, Amy is in the midst of reinventing herself and moving to the next level of her career in the new-media business. No doubt she'll take the advice she offers to all young women searching for budding careers in IT: "Be bold—know who you really are and what you really want—go get it!"

But as a true agent provocateur, Amy admits, "I'm happy with who I am and who I am becoming. And happy to break down a few barriers along the way."

Ellie Rubin
"I Entrepreneur"
www.ellierubin.com

Entrepreneurs in this new millennium won't try to define entrepreneurship as "female" or "male," says Ellie Rubin. Rather, they'll learn how to embrace the necessary balance between the best of female and male traits, with one goal in mind: to win. Ellie shares the secrets behind her successes in the world of IT, and the insights she's gained as cofounder of The Bulldog Group, an international software company that has raised more than $20 million (US) in outside investment and made market waves from Hollywood to Silicon Valley.

High school. 1989. *Decision day.* Ellie Rubin is faced with a choice. Music? Drama? She can either commit to earning a music teacher's degree, or she can choose to shoulder the job as director of this year's school play. To appreciate the

gravity of this high school day of decision, you should know a few things. You should know that Ellie has studied classical music for eight years now. She's trudged off to music lessons every Tuesday night, and now she's good. Very good. She coaxes Chopin nocturnes from the piano and can spin through a Bach prelude on the harpsichord, filtering beautiful pieces from her fingers to an audience's ear. But is she really meant to be a professional pianist? For that matter, can she really direct a play?

Flash forward to 10 months later: a buzzer signals the end of class and the school hallway fills with students. Ask them who Arthur Miller is and most shrug their shoulders. They don't know the name of the man who wrote *Death of a Salesman*, or that Miller married Marilyn Monroe and cast a light on that troubled marriage in his play entitled *After the Fall*. But these same students are wearing After the Fall pins. They know their fellow student, Ellie Rubin, is directing a play by that name. And they know they don't want to miss it.

A hallway full of After the Fall pins was likely the first sign that Ellie, at an early age, already understood and appreciated the power of belonging, the significance of branding, and the impact of one person's entrepreneurial prowess. "We created pins, T-shirts, and posters to generate excitement about the play well before it debuted," Ellie says, sitting years later in the boardroom of The Bulldog Group, the company she cofounded in 1991 with her partner and husband Christopher Strachan. "It was our way of getting the word of mouth around. We sensed that if we could get people to want to 'belong' to the 'After the Fall' following, we'd have a success on our hands." Ellie applied that notion of belonging to build a cast and crew, as well as to attract an audience. "We held special workshops and extra rehearsals that not only focused on acting but also allowed the group to foster a sense of belonging to a special cast—a culture that was key to creating a final product that went far beyond the script and the scene changes."

In the middle of this reminiscence, Ellie's dog, Lola, wanders past on the way to her water bowl in the reception area. Not far from Lola's dish sits another bowl, this one filled with press-on tattoos and dog tags. Anyone who enters or exits Bulldog's offices has to fight off the temptation to dive in and grab one of these neon-bright marketing baubles. Ellie understands that urge. Her insights and appreciation of how marketing, human nature, and technology merge have propelled both Ellie and Bulldog forward in the business of new media design and digital media software.

The Bulldog Group began in 1991 as a marketing communications and design firm—with a twist: all design and customer interaction were facilitated by computer technology. Ellie recalls this decision was made "at a time when this was not the norm," and from this convergence of design and technology Bulldog was able not only to save clients time and money but to show how technology, design, and marketing processes were merging. The company, she says, soon morphed into Canada's leading multimedia production house.

One reason Bulldog's been successful is that it has always been willing to take risks and challenge customers to adopt new ideas and new technologies that were "ahead of the curve," says Ellie. Bulldog began with very few clients who were willing to invest in multimedia production, but the company invested in talented programmers and digital designers as part of its approach to R&D. The approach let it stay on top of the latest technological capabilities and digital design trends, she says. "Taking the risk to invest in resources that fully utilized technology and design helped the company understand issues involved in managing huge amounts of digital files—such as video clips, animation cells, graphics, photos, and audio files— that were typically used in designing a client's Web site or multimedia presentation."

That, in the end, became the genesis for the creation of The Bulldog Group's content management software solution, which is now sold internationally to broadcasting, entertainment, and interactive service providers. Empowered with millions of digital assets and intellectual properties, these media-rich companies are searching for ways not only to streamline internal processes but to capitalize on the intrinsic value of their assets. Recognizing the emerging new business in e-commerce, business-to-business, and business-to-consumer opportunities, they are turning to companies like Bulldog to leverage their existing assets and implement core infrastructure technologies that provide more efficient ways to reuse, re-purpose, and distribute assets.

Ellie estimates that by 2005, the digital media management software and services market could generate more than $2 billion (US) in revenue. Studies have shown that people in those market areas may spend more than 10 percent of their time fruitlessly searching out in-house computer files, and Ellie has estimated that the market for Bulldog's product is already in the $200-million range, and growing fast.

Branding has always been a vital element behind Ellie's vocational success. Bulldog was chosen as the company's name because it reflected an icon that's tenacious, aggressive, and strong—yet whimsical. And that's a pretty good description of the woman herself. Ellie came to the world of IT by a circuitous route: studying English and theater at McGill University in Montreal. Both areas of study were great preparation for business: "I learned to speak, write, and get up on stage—all essential skills for any entrepreneur." Ellie says she's created her own version of networking, which she calls "championship": "By creating what I call circles of coincidence and purposeful collision, I'm able to do business with influencers and decision-makers who will support my ideas, up and down hierarchies and across a broad range of industries." Her networking abilities have played a significant role in laying essential professional groundwork with key technology partners and heavyweight U.S. IT industry players such as Silicon Graphics and Oracle.

Ellie dislikes drawing gender-specific lines when discussing entrepreneuring and information technology. Her advice to anyone looking to break into the IT world is universal, non-gender specific. In *Bulldog: Spirit of the New Entrepreneur*, Ellie encourages her readers to focus on opening doors as a "generalist," then closing the deal as a "specialist." IT companies are looking for those who exude flexibility and agility in their ability to transport skills and accumulate a wide range of hands-on experience. Figure out what you stand for and be flexible in what you can deliver, is Ellie's advice. Today's market is constantly evolving; you have to be able to navigate the chaos and accept the fact that you may end up in a very different place than you originally intended. Along the way you will learn a lot, and you may just be happily surprised at your final destination, she says. The new digital economy requires players who are adaptable, responsive to change, and who possess a portfolio of experience that reflects a professional with the ability to incorporate risk, manage calculated intuition, and maintain a level of stamina—all vital for success today.

For instance, Ellie sees a trend among companies in the software industry: "They're hiring people from different disciplines with a more generalized business background who can actually understand how to bring technology into a business context. Today, there are lots of companies that are now getting investors to invest in a company that's a hybrid of products and services. Well, three years ago, you couldn't get an investor to talk to you if you used the word 'service.' And now they are recognizing that often technological solutions and products require a certain level of customization and consultation, and the product/service combination can be a winning revenue formula."

She believes people considering careers in IT and new media should concentrate less on what job category they feel they'd fit into, and more on what kinds of companies reflect their values. "To 'entrepreneur' as a verb begins by accumulating experience as a means of understanding what you want to do, and then applying a methodical and meticulous plan to acquire the skills you'll need to succeed. Companies breed different cultures, and the products or services that roll out of companies reflect their culture," says Ellie. "Being smart—or having an engineering degree—is not enough . . . In the technology world, [companies] don't know where things are going to end up. You're not sure which side of the world you're going to be on—even in terms of services versus products." These companies need people with a breadth of skills and talents, who can open doors to a variety of client situations, and who have the flexibility to create sales opportunities. Often, when you get trained as a specialist, Ellie says, flexibility is lost in the training: you don't know how to deal with off-the-cuff situations, how to respond creatively, how to deal with things that don't have a formula attached.

Ellie's own knowledge of technology has been largely self-taught, and her experience in business has come from past sales and marketing jobs. Coming from a non-computer industry background is a real advantage, she believes: she learned from experience, and experience builds expertise. Ellie had the foresight to establish offices in the Silicon Valley in 1995 after Apple Computer Corp.—a Bulldog client at the time—kept urging her to come to California and use Apple office space as a base from which to "evangelize" the corporate multimedia market there. The timing was perfect, and Ellie used her strong networking and relationship-building skills to create key Silicon Valley alliances. Since then, The Bulldog Group has built up international markets for its software product in the entertainment, broadcast, and publishing industries with offices in San Francisco, L.A., New York, Toronto, and London.

For entrepreneurs, reinvention is a way of life, and

having grown Bulldog from a fairly traditional marketing and design service business into a leader in the rapidly expanding content management software industry, Ellie has successfully reinvented herself from software company president to author, international speaker, journalist, and media personality. Through her new company, Ellie Corporation, she focuses on writing and speaking to audiences on the subjects of branding, entrepreneurship, and creating sustainable cultures in the world of technology and new media. Ellie Corporation's first publishing venture produced a bestseller in Canada (*Bulldog: Spirit of the New Entrepreneur*), which is being distributed in the U.S., and will soon be published in China. Now at work on a second book, she also pens a weekly column for a Canadian newspaper [*Ambition*] and, on the international speaking circuit, addresses audiences ranging from the corporate crowd at IBM to students at Yale University and the American Film Institute. Ellie says she's also taken on a select number of clients—"either coaching CEOs directly, or assisting them in their ability to attract investment through marketing, branding, and creating sustainable corporate cultures."

Her advice to those looking to blaze new trails in a world increasingly shaped by technology is to resist the temptation to categorize yourself. Keep a generalist's approach to building your portfolio of experience. That includes your approach to the role technology may play in your career: "Just because you might not be interested in engineering or science or math per se, your communications, sales, business, or strategic skills could be the catalyst for your leadership role in the technology industry because of how you adapt, and adopt, technology into a business context. Finding new ways to define success and differentiate one's personal brand is key to finding one's true entrepreneurial spirit."

In her book, Ellie uses the term "independent percolation"

to describe that moment when a person realizes exactly what they want to do. "When you realize that you have accumulated a certain amount of experience and knowledge and . . . that you're willing to make the sacrifices and investment required to build something that reflects your values, you are in a sense ready to move on." She thinks that moment of clarity may come from taking a wide perspective initially, and suggests people begin their career paths by working for "beside-the-point" companies—particularly when they first get out of school and begin their job hunt. "Beside the point" companies is by no means a derogatory term, she says: it identifies often smaller firms that can afford employees the opportunity to gain exposure and experience that is hard to get at a larger organization. In beside-the-point companies, you learn how to be indispensable, how to make decisions that are "close to the skin," she says. "Once you have that experience, you can grow with a smaller company or choose to join a larger organization, as a mature businessperson. In a sense, you have a truly transportable skill."

In her twenties, Ellie felt an intuitive appreciation for what her future held. She recalls walking into a preliminary meeting for a job interview at one of the biggest ad agencies in Canada armed with a strong belief that she possessed the skills and experience desired. When the company president asked her to describe herself in a single sentence, Ellie said: "'I'm a professional eclectic.' And I thought: 'That's great, that's what I am: I am a professional but I have a broad range of interests and capabilities.'" She didn't get the job. The company president said he didn't have room in his company for that kind of flexibility. "He was very clear about it. He said: 'I wouldn't know how to pay you. I wouldn't know how to promote you. And it will cause a revolution in my organization, because you don't fit the mold.'" Ellie remembers feeling totally shocked. She could have left feeling disappointed. Desperate. Instead, a different emotion took hold. "I came out of that [meeting] feeling cheated, but at the same time, I thought: 'You know what? There are people who are going to want me exactly because of this.'" Ellie remains a professional eclectic, someone with an innate understanding of what it takes to create a place to which others are drawn to belong. She reflects the entrepreneurial spirit in the new millennium, and its winning ways.

Jennifer Stewart

Brand Manager
Yahoo! Canada
www.yahoo.ca

Jennifer Stewart, 31, loves marketing products that have exciting potential. That quality has always driven her career choices, and it was that particular passion that led to her current position as brand manager for Yahoo! Canada.

Like others in the high-tech industry, Jennifer had never heard of a job like hers when she was in high school, because the concept of "branding" simply didn't exist and Yahoo! was just a gleam in the eye of two brainy American computer geeks. But Jennifer knew she loved advertising, and her degrees in commerce and international business were her first steps toward her goal of eventually owning and operating her own ad agency. Nevertheless, the technological revolution forced Jennifer's career to take a slightly different turn.

Her first job in technology was with the MIJO Corporation—a production, duplication, and distribution arm for motion picture distributors in Canada. In her position there, she formed strategic alliances with broadcasters and publishers to implement digital networks for the high-speed delivery of advertising material. This foray into the

Jennifer writes, "**ISDN** is a digital, dedicated phone line with a broader bandwidth than a regular phone line. At MIJO, we used ISDN as part of a digital ad-transmission system to some Canadian newspaper publishers."

realm of technology was a thrilling experience, as Jennifer began to learn about using fiber optics and ISDN technology. These technology breakthroughs in information delivery were hugely important to the studios, which were limited to short turnaround times in "Canadianizing" advertising material. Before the high-tech solutions came into play, the industry was dependent on couriers for delivery and experienced the inevitable headaches of holdups at Customs.

While working within the high-tech field, Jennifer became impressed with Internet start-ups such as PointCast Network and Yahoo! well before she joined these companies in a marketing capacity. Yahoo.com was the first online navigational guide to the Web, and as a user Jennifer admired the company's "human qualities"; that is, she felt that the Yahoo! interface helped to make her computer more accessible, easier to use, and almost "friendly."

Now, as a member of the Yahoo! Canada team, Jennifer manages all marketing and communications for the Canadian arm of the hip American-based company. She develops innovative brand-positioning programs to strengthen mass consumer appeal and build brand awareness and traffic on the Web site. Along with a production team, she also creates traffic and revenue-generating opportunities and extends the Yahoo! Canada brand through strategic partnerships and co-ventures. According to Jennifer, one of the challenges of being a brand manager is "'marketing' to other departments to justify her budget because spending money will always take a backseat to revenue-generating departments." But that challenge is offset by the opportunity to work with "other marketing gurus and product developers to create the voice that speaks to our consumer."

Jennifer adds that Yahoo!'s culture is critical to her enjoyment of her position. Like many new-media companies, Yahoo! promotes an entrepreneurial spirit with a strong sense of team built on self-reliant members. Jennifer claims there's also an advantage to working in Canada because "the industry here is still relatively small and there is an opportunity to make a name for yourself, particularly if you're a woman." She also urges those considering careers in new media to seek a company that offers creative compensation packages and encourages new players to try to own a piece of the business through stock options.

As a woman in a male-dominated industry, Jennifer also feels that she brings an important perspective to her team. "I bring the perspective of a female consumer, someone who wants a useful, relevant, and dynamic tool. Sometimes it is as simple as saying, 'I don't get this. What benefit does this feature provide for our users?' I also play a role in developing branding strategies and how a product is positioned and introduced to consumers." Jennifer also recommends joining communities such as Wired Woman Society and Webgrrls International to form alliances and build friendships.

So where does Jennifer see herself five years down the cyber path? "I will still be having fun, working hard, creating innovative marketing campaigns for a dynamic Internet company." Proving her passion for marketing again and again.

"Brandardized"

Twenty years ago we would never have said that Royal Bank was a brand—it was simply a place where we "kept" our money. Xerox was simply a machine that duplicated our documents. Kleenex was a tissue that we wiped our noses with. But, in hindsight these are all brands that subtly became household names without the end-user ever really knowing how the effects of marketing and branding influenced their purchasing decisions.

Today, we as consumers and users are enveloped by information overload. New products are entering the marketplace at a remarkable pace and there is an intense competition for consumer attention. The traditional steps of "brand building" are out the window and the new buzzword is "relationship marketing." Because the Internet has created a global "marketing nirvana," companies now have access to critical consumer information—gathered directly from the source—and they can use that personal information to forge "relationships" with the user. In addition, Web-based companies can now customize for a specific consumer's needs instead of relying on old-style marketing methods that blindly try to reach mass markets. Many traditional brands have been slow on the uptake of the "Internet invasion" of retail. Some companies have even chosen to ignore the effects the Internet will have on their businesses. While it is widely speculated that the dotcom hype is exactly that, there is no denying the fact that billions of dollars have been spent online this year. Those online sales are being scooped from a bricks and mortar location somewhere.

As opposed to the North American "24-hour society" where consumers can buy anytime or anywhere, Europeans have staunchly maintained their focus on culture, family, and balance. Family food and supplies can only be purchased within the hours of 9–5 p.m. except on Thursday evenings, which is "late shopping night." Occasionally the late night consumer might be able to find a "Nite Shop" that is open until midnight, but you may as well forget it if you think any European is going to work all night to keep her or his shop open to sell a couple of liters of milk. Life is too short for that!

Globalization and the Internet may take its toll on the laid-back European lifestyle as large American conglomerates slowly make in-roads to European culture and more companies conduct business online. But, as a North American expatriate living in Amsterdam, make no mistake about it, I will be the first one running down to the WalMart in my Reebok's to load up on Q-tips, Playtex Tampons, and Ziploc sandwich bags!

Shari Swan,
Reebok International
Amsterdam, the Netherlands

Zina Kaye

Partner, House of Laudanum
Managing Director, Agent All-Black Ltd.
Chairman, Anti-Destination Society
http://Laudanum.net

The next time you're invited to a dinner party, think of
Zina Kaye, whose interest in technology and the Internet
was spawned over a lot of music and bad cooking in 1992.

Zina was working as a journalist in Australia when she
attended a dinner party with her housemates and met
Sandra Davey, a woman who introduced her to GreenNet,
cyberfeminism, and the power of the Internet. She was
working on a campaign for Amnesty International and was
known as one of the few people around with an email
account she could actually use. Zina then became intrigued
by the prospect of using the Internet as a tool for activism.

Soon after the dinner party, Zina enrolled in a bachelor of
fine arts program at the University of New South Wales and
moved into a house with a Mac
developer and two traditional
activists. The four students dug
deep into the social protocols of
the Internet. They decided that if
the Internet was going to change
the world, it was a great place to
experiment with gender, sexuality, presence, communication,
and spatiality. It was the perfect
time for online experimentation,

DOBRILA STAMENKOVIC FROM
THE MUSEUM STATION SERIES

so, as Zina puts it, she "got a modem and started hassling people with it."

Before moving to Australia, Zina had actually followed a more traditional career path, working in journalism and doing film script development before becoming the editor of a high-profile London-based magazine. But she didn't like the status quo, felt frustrated about being forced to use big words to talk about small concepts, and decided to go back to school and build a career outside the corporate sphere.

CUseeMe is an Internet-based multi-user chat and video conferencing tool that allows people to communicate with each other face to face or in group discussions through a personal computer. This software product is commonly used in education and business environments, where collaboration is an asset to learning.

Nicole Goodman

Principal, Technical Lead

www.neurofunk.com

Before she graduated from the University of New South Wales, Zina realized her computer savvy would make it possible for her to make a living without joining a traditional business. In fact, even as a student she began freelancing and found herself with the freedom to explore whatever projects seemed intriguing. She earned a living teaching people how to set up their computers with modems and how to use the Internet.

She was also very lucky to have an inspiring tutor early in her exploration. Bill Seaman, one of her professors at UNSW, encouraged her to play on the Internet and create Web sites, even before Mosaic was released. While most other multimedia designers were working on CD-ROM projects, Zina was able to explore the medium of the future. She recalls when Seaman gave her class the task of writing an imaginary resume outlining their careers 10 years down the road. Zina wrote that she would own a satellite and several airplanes, but couldn't have imagined

Text-based virtual worlds or "**MUD**s" began as multi-player adventure games in the late 1970s. In fact, the word "MUD" stands for "Multi-User Dungeon"—multi-user versions of the classic Infocom computer game Dungeon. In the early 1990s, the use of these environments began to expand to educational and business applications. One particularly popular kind of MUD is "MOO." MOO stands for "MUD Object Oriented." The MOO software was originally written by Stephen White (then an undergraduate) and more fully developed by Pavel Curtis (then of Xerox PARC). MOO is more easily end-user programmable than most other MUD software, and some of the most exciting innovations in this field have been developed in MOO as a result.

Amy Bruckman

Assistant Professor

College of Computing

Georgia Institute of Technology

that less than a decade later she would be using the Internet to tie satellites and airplanes together.

As well as seeing electronic arts as the perfect place to develop her playful imagination, Zina was insightful enough to see that there was much more than fun and games going on online. She saw the value of integrating one system or device with another and realized that there would always be a need for people like her to devise interfaces between seemingly mutually exclusive objects.

It's hard to even keep track of all the projects Zina is involved with. As proof of her passion for process and learning, she has learned how to build airplanes so that she can now work to develop robotic controls for an airplane that people will be able to fly over the Internet. As a successful (although admittedly unconventional) businessperson, she sits on the boards of several companies, travels the world as a guest speaker, and still makes time to manage experimental servers and host a radio show called *Hydrogen Jukebox*, which features her own mix of combustible experimental radio.

It's clear that flexibility and variety are important to
Zina, as is an open, comfortable working environment
that encourages experimentation and mutual support.
There's a meeting room at the front of her studio that is
painted dark blue and looks out through big windows to
the sea. People can eat, drink, relax, and read there, or
linger around the other nooks and crannies of the studio,
leaning against cupboards, resting on piles of cushions, or
watching a TV that sits on a perch next to the vending
machine.

Zina also values the flexibility that she finds online. She's
very aware of the gender difference in places such as MOOs
and other virtual community hubs that she uses for technical support, and responds to this by capitalizing on the flexibility of identity on the Internet. As a social experiment
she regularly changes her own online identity.

In fact, almost everything Zina does online is an experiment of one kind or another. One of her favorites was a
performance work she called "Liftworld," which took place
in 1996, just as the Internet was starting to fulfill its potential as a place where people from around the world could
gather and communicate. Zina invited artists to perform an
event that would be broadcast over the Internet via
CUseeMe. All the artists took the persona of the Agent All
Black, who became a metaphor for moving to another place
. . . Warsaw. The piece actually became a love story of sorts
between Zina, her counterparts, and some artists in Poland.
On the performance night they built a set, joined some
footage together, and created a fantastical space that was
completely seamless. It was an exercise in folding space that
left the audience unsure as to what was real and what
wasn't. A man falling naked down some stairs, a woman
painted like an elevator unzipping her body, a bunch of

aliens in wheelchairs letting off fireworks—it all became one place.

"Liftworld," like everything Zina does online, was experimental and collaborative, and pushed the Internet into new spaces and places we can all explore.

Farah Perelmuter

Speakers' Spotlight
www.speakers.ca

When Farah Perelmuter first started her speakers' bureau in 1995, the fresh-faced former advertising executive thought having a Web site address on her business card would give her credibility. "The URL was so long that I didn't think anyone would ever remember it, but I thought it looked cool! At the time I wasn't sure if anything would come of the Internet. Little did I know . . ." Today, Farah, 25, is CEO of Speakers' Spotlight, an agency that represents a virtual who's who of professional and celebrity speakers, and she considers the Web site [**www.speakers.ca**] to be her most important business tool.

"Our Web site receives hundreds of thousands of hits and generates a huge volume of business. We have the world's most comprehensive digital library of speaker videos, which allows our clients instant access to potential

speakers like Rubin 'Hurricane' Carter, Silken Laumann, comedian Dave Broadfoot, astronaut Roberta Bondar, Joan Rivers, Christopher Reeve, and media mogul Moses Znaimer." The Web site and digital video library have been instrumental in helping the agency land high-profile gigs such as a recent presentation by Nicholas Negroponte, director of MIT's media lab, who received a fee of $40,000 (US) for his one-time appearance.

Farah owns and operates the company along with her business partner and husband, Martin, a corporate lawyer. She quips that when she decided to start her own business, she "couldn't afford a lawyer so she decided to marry one." Both left their high-pressure jobs in June 1995 to form Speakers' Spotlight. "Within that one month, we got married, we moved, we quit our jobs, and we started the business. Our families and friends thought we were crazy!" Nevertheless, the Perelmuters prudently decided to embrace entrepreneurialism completely debt-free. "We saved and bought everything we needed, so we'd start with no debt. It cost us about $25,000, and we slowly saved that money by sacrificing perks, staying at home, eating in, and not taking vacations."

The agency slowly acquired top-notch inspirational speakers, but Farah says at the beginning she was often caught off guard when certain celebrities came on board, particularly those of sports fame. "Stereotypically, women don't know anything about sports. Well, I'm afraid I helped prove that one correct! One day I got a call from someone named Paul asking for Martin. I put him on hold and told Martin the call was for him. I said, 'There's someone holding for you, named Paul something. Oh yeah, his last name is Henderson.' When I saw Martin's face (and the fact that he practically flew out of his chair to grab the phone), I knew this guy must be a 'somebody.' I had no idea that Paul Henderson is a national hockey hero, having scored the winning goal in the 1972 series against Russia!"

Farah also admits that she still gets a little "starstruck" when dealing with some celebrities on the company's roster. "Another time I answered the phone and had a wonderful conversation with a woman named Margaret. We talked about working with our husbands and all that it entails. She mentioned that, even today, she's still referred to as Margaret Trudeau. Okay, needless to say, although I sounded very professional and calm on the phone, I danced like crazy around the room! I couldn't believe that I was speaking with Pierre Trudeau's ex-wife 'Maggie.' We signed her on as one of our speakers and have had the pleasure to get to know her personally."

When the Perelmuters asked clients how they could help them pick speakers, the response was "Let us see the speakers in action." Now their video library can showcase the speakers in actual presentation mode. Users can also click on bio information, check out speaker schedules, and email specific questions. Farah says that in today's chaotic and fast-paced world, her clients need access to instant information. "Taking advantage of today's powerful technology makes my job easier and more efficient."

Farah says the Internet has revolutionized her business, and she looks forward to exploring new technologies in an effort to increase revenue and the quality of her service. She also intends to use the Internet for research so as not to be caught off guard when the next sports hero signs up with Speakers' Spotlight.

If the idea hasn't been thought of, conceive it. If the technology doesn't exist, build it.
This Media Lab work ethic inspired me to take impossible ideas and build real technologies. From designing interactive toys to digitally enhancing children's television, I create innovations that help people explore and explain events in the world around them.

Tamara Lackner

M.S., Media Arts & Sciences

MIT Media Lab

Heather Gordon

Online Advertising Sales Manager
CityInteractive, CHUM Television
www.cityinteractive.com

Like many employees at Toronto's trendy television station,
28-year-old Heather Gordon kicked off her career as a
volunteer, despite a degree in media arts. Because of the
intense internal job competition, her first nonpaying job
was as "CHUM camera girl"—that is, she walked around
with an instant camera taking snaps of party guests during
star-studded media events and schmooze-fests, until someone took notice. She was among a number of fresh faces at
CHUM vying for a position on-camera, but she soon grew
charmed by the power of new media and took a behind-
the-scenes career path.

Eventually, her constant presence in the hip CHUM
building paid off (not monetarily) when another internship
position as administrative coordinator opened up in the

freshly launched CityInteractive
department. With that opportunity, Heather's cyber career was
officially cast.

Through hard work (a second
job and not a lot of sleep), her
position as administrative coordinator progressed to paying work
as online sales assistant, online
sales rep, and finally sales
manager. That career course took

four years, and Heather says she now has a position she would never have imagined, since her job didn't exist even five years ago. Her current role as online sales manager requires a continual effort to create integrated ways of selling TV and the Web as one package. Heather's responsibility is to generate sales revenue for all the CHUM Web sites (MuchMusic, MuchMoreMusic, Space, Star, and Bravo!) and to keep finding innovative ways to incorporate advertisers into the content of the Web sites.

She praises her accidental career choice and cites endless professional opportunities now available in online sales. "There were definitely benefits for getting into online sales relatively early. The obvious advantage is less competition. When our division needed to hire a sales rep, there wasn't a stack of resumes from qualified people on hand. I just worked very hard to fill the role and not give [CHUM] a reason to go looking elsewhere to hire."

From "camera girl" to "cyber girl," Heather is currently poised on the cutting edge of a cool career in cyber sales, and as a result she's no longer willing to work for free. Now her motto could be, "Show me the e-money!"

Catherine Warren

Chief Operating Officer
Blue Zone Entertainment Inc.
www.bluezone.com

As a computer journalist, Catherine Warren spent half a decade or so chasing down technology stories, attending trade shows, and interviewing tech creators and tech users—in the U.S. and beyond. "Combining technology and publishing, science and writing, was a natural extension of my life," says Catherine, who has been recognized by publications and national organizations as a new-media pioneer. She wrote her master's thesis on ways to combine technology and creativity; founded in-house magazines for Sun Microsystems, Hewlett-Packard, and Unisys; was team and operations planner for Microsoft's multimedia science encyclopedia (which evolved into *Encarta*); and served as editor or publisher of more than 25 books and magazine series on science and computing.

While doing her undergraduate degree in physics at Reed College in Portland, Oregon, in the early 1980s, she learned to program in UNIX and PASCAL, and then moved on to Columbia University Graduate School of Journalism in 1985 for her master's in science writing. "For me, computers were the link to a whole world of technology

JEROME KASHETSKY

reporting and journalism. . . . As a computer journalist, I was like the *paparazzo*—and the technology was the celebrity.

"I got into computers early and was one of the first college students to test the Apple 'Lisa'—the early Mac.

"When I was a graduate student at Columbia University, wanting to write my thesis on the infancy of multimedia in 1984, I was told, 'There's no story there.' Well, not only was there a story, but the story turned out to be one of the biggest stories of the latter half of the century! I wrote my version of the story for my thesis, regardless of the naysaying faculty. And since that time, I've kept my nose for news and for new-media innovation."

Catherine believes the machine can be an extension of the mind. As a multimedia producer and publisher, she spent another half decade or so hiring and inspiring teams to capitalize on technology's creative potential.

And today? She's responsible for the day-to-day operations of Blue Zone as one of three officers in a company that's leading the convergence of mass media and new media. What does Blue Zone have planned for the new century? The focus is on development of a landmark news and information site via an interactive television-and-broadband development agreement with a national television network.

UNIX is not a group of castrated men but a freeware operating system developed in the 1960s and commonly used on workstations and in networking environments.

PASCAL is an early, high-level programming language named after a dead European mathematician. "High level" suggests (believe it or not) that it is closer to human than machine language.

Alissa Antle
Senior Producer
Brainium.com

She says Blue Zone's platform and strategic services will be used to produce television programming and personalized news-on-demand for a national TV network, a 24-hour headline news channel, and to simulcast interactive content on-air and online.

The plan is for viewers to see headline news while being able to simultaneously access a wealth of related information online. To facilitate this, the network—CTV—plans to hire a team of "Web publishers to monitor live news and to file a steady stream of fresh, headline-related content so that CTVNews.com surfers can get information as it happens."

Her brother Bruce is Blue Zone's CEO; he says the company is "out to end the couch potato revolution" by converting passive television viewers into active online consumers. And CTV Inc. is a great place to start that conversion: in addition to the CTV Television Network, it owns an independent TV station, six affiliate stations, and a regional cable network, plus has ownership interest in five specialty channels.

"Bruce and I have a great professional relationship based on tremendous mutual respect, a strong, family-ingrained work ethic, and clear division of responsibilities," says Catherine. And while Bruce's relationship with technology has always been very hands-on ("He took apart a transistor radio when he was eight, and converted it into a metal detector"), Catherine's tie to technology was linked to "publishing." Catherine recalls producing neighborhood "newspapers" and other projects with her girlfriends, and printing personal poetry booklets in her youth.

Catherine, who considers her mother an early new-media pioneer and personal inspiration, says her relationship with technology continues to evolve. One dimension of that evolution will be realized through her young son. "Dakota will no doubt grow up in a world of mind-blowing technological advances," says Catherine. "My husband and I will do what we can to give Dakota exposure to other cultures, a sense of compassion, and (an appreciation for) the natural world."

He will certainly have access to all the best technological tools, she says. "But what he elects to do with them will largely depend on his relationship with people and with the planet . . . My hope for him is that he contributes to making these tools make a difference for humanity."

Sang Mah

Cofounder and Chief Operating Officer
Credo Interactive Inc.—The Character Motion Company
www.charactermotion.com

Sang Mah has always been smart and she's always been curious. As an undergraduate she was smart enough to receive a computer science degree with a minor in business. And she was smart enough to do a master of science in computing, completing her thesis in computer animation and artificial intelligence (AI). But it was her curiosity that brought Sang to her current role as the chief operating officer of Credo Interactive, a company she cofounded that develops innovative 3-D character animation solutions for use in entertainment, education, business, and the arts.

Sang's first technology job was actually as an undergraduate lab assistant for a physical chemistry professor: she was responsible for running computer analysis programs. It was this job that first exposed Sang to invention and to a blue-

print-free work environment that encouraged exploration. She loved the crazy apparatus built by the scientists, and really enjoyed being encouraged to innovate.

But Sang wasn't too crazy about the dark basement she worked in. She also wasn't thrilled with her second technology job working in the accounting department of a large forestry company as part of a university co-op program. As much as she was drawn to the opportunities for advancement that were available there, Sang knew right away that she wanted to do something different and that she wanted to make big things happen.

Even though she had a strong academic background, it wasn't until Sang combined computing with her other interests that she really got excited about what she could do with technology. For Sang, it was the mating of computing with the arts that really made software come alive. She had always been passionate about entertainment, dance, and education, and was suddenly sure that software was really just a new kind of clay that she could use to invent something that would be valuable for dancers and educators.

And so Sang decided to delve into information technology and new media. With her computer science background, she had a lot to offer and decided to explore this new arena by becoming a volunteer. She searched around her community to find ways to donate her time, and chose to take on roles teaching computer skills to teenage single mothers and immigrant women. She also volunteered as the coproducer of a short animated film.

Getting involved in film and animation reignited Sang's desire to bring more visual depth to computing, and so the move toward computer graphics seemed logical. The allure of dance and motion eventually led her to form an academic research group called Life Forms, which conducted research into the modeling and animation of human figures. Her desire to bring this technology to industry then led Sang to spin off Credo Interactive Inc. for the commercialization of Life Forms and other motion and animation technologies.

Being in a start-up software company brought together the love of invention Sang had developed in the chemistry lab, her passion for dance and the arts, and her educational background in computer science. It also added the element of entrepreneurship that made it possible for Sang to live up to her endless drive to make things happen. At Credo, Sang enjoys being challenged by the diversity of roles and responsibilities she has set out for herself. As the chief operating officer of Credo, she is responsible for leading and managing product development, research, and production in a constantly evolving company.

As a principal of Credo, Sang's contributions don't end there. She is responsible for contributing to the development and implementation of the company's corporate strategy, and, as a key leader at the company, it is also her job to be as inspiring and focused as she possibly can be. Sang often feels that her role at Credo is to be the "glue" that keeps all the projects and teams on track, and so she works hard to help her teams find success where they thought success was impossible, and to deliver products they can be proud of.

Sang's job extends outside the walls of the Credo office as well. As the COO of a technology company, she takes seriously her responsibility to have a positive effect on the way technology is developed. She wants to build technology applications that can improve computing as well as improving the world outside the desktop. To do this Sang spends a lot of time listening to her customers and understanding the market. For example, because Life Forms has its roots in choreography, Sang spends time in the dance and dance education community, making sure her software product makes sense to the customers it was designed for.

Sang admits that new media is still a predominantly male arena, but she firmly believes that the door is wide open for women to make their mark. "New media and technology careers offer women the potential for incredible financial reward, flexibility, and career satisfaction," Sang says with her quiet poise and almost uncanny confidence. "You have to be confident in your abilities and insights, and realize that if the solution isn't obvious to you, then it probably isn't obvious at all."

Sang knows that new-media industries are in desperate need of people with characteristics traditionally attributed to women. She knows from experience that the industry needs communicative, organized, intuitive workers at all levels who can thrive in a world where there aren't any blueprints to follow and where everyone is looking for their own path.

Natasha Kong and Nicole Blades

SheNetworks
www.shenetworks.com

Shebytes! founders Natasha Kong and Nicole Blades are two women with a hearty appetite for new media. With their already successful ezine and the recent launch of their online lifestyle network aimed at women, the dynamic duo are taking a bite out of mainstream and male-dominated approaches to technology.

In 1998, the pair first launched Shebytes!, an online new-media magazine that looks at how technology touches the everyday lives of everyday women. Natasha and Nicole claim they created the ezine to help women stay "in the know and in the now," with features and stories written in a style that, like the content, is informative but also sharp, witty, and biting. Their ezine tag line is "*Shebytes!* a new media mouthful," and Natasha and Nicole admit that reaction to their debut site gave them a craving for more new-media projects. Next on the

menu was SheNetworks, an online community companion and resource hub that follows women through their lives, from age 13 to 34. It is a unique hybrid—part magazine and part networked community—consisting of branded Internet sites serving the needs of the wired women of a generation that identify being online with being in line with what's happening in their ever-changing environment. Natasha and Nicole claim that SheNetworks is all about "content, community, communication, and, above all, convenience."

But who are the women behind this fledgling female-focused new-media enterprise? Twenty-something Natasha and Nicole have fashioned their business through sheer hard work, willpower—and a little karma. The pair met in Toronto when Nicole was looking for work in Canada after a long stint in Barbados and the U.S. She needed to revamp her resume, and through a shared connection she linked up with Natasha for design advice. The two soon realized they shared a secret desire to produce a magazine aimed at women. That was the click. Before long, they had fleshed out plans for Shebytes!, and less than a year later the concept for SheNetworks was born.

With Natasha's inherent artistic esthetic and strong design sense, and Nicole's writing flair, they are the consummate creative couple. As a team, they have an instant synergy that stems from shared philosophy, values, and fighting spirit, firmly rooted in their diverse backgrounds.

Natasha was born in Vancouver to parents of mixed Chinese descent. Although Natasha's father, an account manager at Nestlé, was continually encouraging her to use computers at an early age, Natasha shunned the cold world of technology and headed straight for the stage. At age 10, she was already acting in live productions in the local Vancouver scene, and by age 14, she was touring with a performing company in Australia. Predictably, Natasha soon forayed into film and television production, and at the same time focused on her emerging artistic sensibility. In her early twenties, Natasha secured a fine arts scholarship at UBC, but quickly became dissatisfied and headed to Toronto armed with paints and portfolio. Then her career took a major turn when she bought a Mac and started dabbling in arts software. Soon she joined forces with Byron Wong to cofound Random Media Core, a new-media creative house. Less than two years after picking up a computer for the first time, Natasha had taught herself graphic design, animation, and 3-D rendering, and had established herself as one of Toronto's premier Web designers. In 1996, *Canadian Business Magazine* dubbed her "a fast-tracker who works wonders on Web sites," and Natasha's new-media career was officially launched.

Meanwhile, Nicole was fast-tracking along a different creative career path. The Montreal-born writer's journey into journalism began with a cheeky piece about hair politics and cold chicken wings for a hometown newspaper. After graduating from York University with two BAs, one in mass communications and the other in psychology, Nicole moved to New York City, and two weeks later was doing PR for the NBC talk show *Sally Jessy Raphael*. Her next stop was *Essence* magazine, where she wrote about the women's fashion scene. Later she moved on to warmer horizons as a features writer for the leading newspaper in Barbados, copping an award for a health feature series along the way. Nicole contends she always had a penchant for working with words and easily justifies her chosen art form: "Everything has a time and space: a reason. Words, for me, define these things. I write to gain reason."

As artist and author respectively, Natasha and Nicole claim their partnership is more than just a creative union. A shared outlook on life and a similar approach to people contribute to their implicit trust in each other's business perspective, especially when making critical decisions regarding vision, strategy, and goals.

Natasha and Nicole confess they've also drawn creative impulse from some unconventional sources, including kung fu and karma. The petite women are avid kung fu fans, and they both contend that studying a martial art together has strengthened their partnership by giving them insight into themselves and each other. Natasha asserts, "The kung fu gives us inner focus and a chance to see things for what they are. It prepares you mentally, physically, and emotionally. It also gives us fighting power and the strength and courage to say, 'You know what? That blow really hurt but we're going to keep on going and work through it.'"

That fighting spirit has been integral to their struggle to build a business from the ground up. Nicole says, "It's been a fever-pitch drive to develop product, raise financing, and forge a team all at the same time." The partners also called on their Chinese-inspired teachings to prepare them for their entrepreneurial education. Natasha says, "We wrote our business plan by ourselves with no previous business training, so it was an incredible learning curve. We would meet with banks and potential financiers only to find we were missing

Valuation
Valuation has a new face for today's entrepreneurs and investors. In a world where key assets are intangible and cash flows aren't necessarily king, non-price valuation has become more of a common practice. Dot-coms and others can take a cue from the non-profit sector. In a world where social impact trumps cash flows, what we value when making an investment decision is the probability that an organization will generate even greater impact as a result of its leadership, strategic partnerships, and innovation.
Kelly Fitzsimmons
Co-Founder
New Profit Inc.

a critical element of our plan, so we would have to revise, re-pitch, and revise again. Kung fu helped us to keep our minds clear and focused throughout that frustrating learning process."

Natasha adds, "Nothing we could ever have read or learned in school could have helped us in our quest to run our own company: write a business plan, shop it around, and raise funding. The world of business and Internet start-ups is driven by a completely different set of tools, language, and terminology." She remembers one of their early meetings with potential investors when they were asked, What's the valuation of your company? The pair was completely unfamiliar with the term and realized quickly they were out of their league—but they've since learned to face uncertainty and even rejection head-on.

Natasha and Nicole have every intention of taking their kung fu philosophy online in their attempt to conquer the competitive real-world computer game. It's not surprising, then, that the pair also share a strong belief in the power of karma. Natasha unabashedly admits, "We definitely believe in karma; that is, whatever you put out there comes back to you. If you put out a negative energy, it'll only come back to hurt you. We try to stay true to that philosophy so we can stay true to ourselves and remain honest and open with the people around us."

Natasha and Nicole try to extend their eastern thinking to their new-media business. Both women agree that they are motivated by people rather than by the technology, and claim they want to balance business with social improvement. Nicole explains, "When it comes down to it, people aren't too concerned with how technology works, but more how it works for them, and SheBytes! delves into that— technology from a social side, not science." Natasha agrees and adds that their particular focus is women because they feel women haven't received the same opportunities afforded to men in the realm of technology. "In the male-dominated arena of digital culture, women are stepping into the game at half-time. Shebytes! helps women get in the game."

The duo also recognizes that most women want technology to be relevant to their lives, and emphasize that technology really underlies all aspects of our lives. They attempt to address that with their content. With a thematic approach, every issue of SheBytes! examines a particular industry and how it has been affected by technology, basically looking at what happens when technology meets real life. Technology has the quiet ability to pop up in the most unexpected places—the music world, wedding industry, agriculture. Natasha claims, "Technology is filling up our plates and Shebytes! will help you digest all there is to know."

What do the SheNetworks women hunger for next? Natasha says they're destined to shape their business beyond the Internet. "We have hopes of SheNetworks going way beyond the Web: a TV show, a print magazine . . . we want to build it and then pass on the torch to someone else and pursue our other dreams." Dreams such as Natasha's consuming desire to start a theater group for young people, and Nicole's hankering to publish her own novel. Anyone who meets the powerful pair will realize they probably haven't taken on more than they can chew.

Liz Sauter: E-business Specialist

Consulting E-Business Solutions Client Representative
IBM Canada Ltd.
www.ibm.ca

Liz Sauter's office is an IBM laptop computer. Her job, like her office, is portable. As a mobile worker, Liz has something many don't have—perspective. For two years, she divvied up her workweek between technology's haves—her corporate clients—and have-nots—specifically, homeless youth and street kids who attended her computer tutorials at a community center. We asked Liz to share her insights, both professional and personal, afforded by her position.

Q: **First, exactly what is e-business? And what does your job entail?**

A: "E-business in its simplest form is [about] transforming key business processes using Internet technologies." Liz works with a team of people who implement e-commerce strategies that will best fit a customer's line of business.

These "solutions" are put together in the form of hardware, software, and services. Her main client is one of Canada's largest banks.

"There is no typical day," says Liz. "One day I'm doing a range of research—analyzing and assessing different areas on the Internet, intranet, extranet that I may be asked to talk about. The

GLAMOURSHOTS

next I'm creating presentations on e-business using multimedia tools, or sharing with my colleagues new and innovative technologies, Web sites—anything that helps us discuss e-business with clients."

Q: **How did you land your job?**

A: "A little bad luck, and a lot of initiative." Her first job in technology was punching health insurance cards in a children's rehabilitation hospital. The hospital's budget dried up and her job was cut. "We were asked not to come to work on Monday. Since I was on my own and needed to pay the rent, I ended up going to a personnel agency to find work." IBM was looking for an administrative assistant. After three interviews, Liz got the job. While working as a secretary, she had to manually create monthly reports identifying where IBM's corporate donations were going. Different executives wanted different versions of the same report. "It took me days to create these. A colleague showed me how he did his reports using a system program. I took the user guide home and automated my reports so I could update and add data from each month, lay out a standard set of reports, and run each off really easily!" That initiative paid off. Today, Liz is part of a team whose responsibilities range from enhancing awareness of e-business solutions at IBM, to devising e-commerce strategies for IBM's clients.

Q: **Is being a mobile worker a good gig?**

A: Liz usually dials into work from her home to get her email to log onto the Internet to do her research. And IBM lets her work a flex-week, so she works four longish days and takes Fridays off. When we caught up with her, however, she was logging more time in the office than usual. "As a mobile worker, you have the advantage of being able to work from anywhere—and I do mean anywhere. Conference rooms, airplanes, someone else's office, or home. Being a mobile worker means working at home with no distractions . . . You get a lot more done,

but being in an office has advantages too . . . You pick up any
conversations that just happen to
be about your customer or team.
And that adds a different dimension and tremendous value,
depending on the type of work
you are doing."

Q: **What did your experience
tutoring street kids teach you?**

A: One day a week, for two
years, Liz could be found neither
at home office nor corporate
bunker. She spent Fridays working as a facilitator of Beat the
Street, and would head to a
community center lab to teach
computer skills. The idea was to
help street kids figure out the
Internet and what's on it—and in
it—for them. Practical skills,
from how to write a resume, to
how to search the Web for jobs
or housing, to tutorials, were the
main focus.

Liz was amazed to discover the
array of Net-related information
and skills-upgrading resources
and programs available for free
via walk-in, community, and social services programs.
"These resources aren't advertised or marketed the way
corporate initiatives are. And there doesn't seem to be an
'end-to-end process' that helps guide the street youths to
specific resources—no one person or site that helps them

understand everything that's available to them." The challenge, she says, "is creating an awareness of what's out there for people's different needs." Liz believes the solution lies in promoting awareness and offering support on a community-by-community basis. One person at a time. One day at a time.

Q: **Any advice to people intimidated by technology?**

A: "Don't be! The first time I sat down at a desk and hooked up, I plugged in the connection cable and kept getting an error message. I shut down the operating system, rebooted over and over again, checked the addresses, etc. Then, finally, I called the help line. They walked me through all the same steps that I had just gone through and then I realized something: I had forgotten to plug the cable into the wall." Approach technology as a learning experience, she suggests. "Act like a kid. Explore your opportunities and community resources. And remember: you can't break anything."

Liz Dunn

Senior Content Manager
Spotlife
www.spotlife.com

Liz Dunn is the senior content manager at **Spotlife.com**, an exciting new start-up that focuses on enabling personal broadcasting on the Web. Until now, would-be broadcasters shared their thoughts with text and images, but as bandwidth has increased, video content has become the newest way to communicate online. Spotlife.com helps new Internet broadcasters to do live, streaming broadcasts, and even hosts webcams for people who want their friends to be able to watch them work.

Until very recently Liz was the senior content producer for the Shopping Channel at Excite@Home. But she once spent a year—an *entire* year—sitting next to Pierre Omidyar (the future founder of eBay), listening to his vision for online auctions. She paid attention to all his ideas, but just

kept thinking to herself that no one was going to want to wade through a site with thousands of people selling their stuff.

Well, sure, Liz wishes she'd bought into Omidyar's ideas about online auctions. But on the other hand she's glad she didn't buy into thousands of *other* ideas she's heard about over coffees and around watercoolers in Silicon

Valley over the past six years. While working as a senior producer at Excite, Liz had plenty of opportunity to gad about Silicon Valley, listening to ideas and watching people adapt to life in what many believe is the hub of technology.

Liz graduated from the University of California at Berkeley with a degree in religious studies. She landed a job at *Emigre*, a renowned design magazine that also creates computer typefaces. This was Liz's first job out of college, so she found herself doing everything from answering phones to proofreading the magazine. She put her writing talent to work and authored a few articles for the publication. And in an early demonstration of her drive and talent, she even designed her own typeface. Liz's font was featured in *Emigre* #16—pretty impressive for someone who didn't even know how to use a computer before she joined the company. In college Liz had typed her essays up on a manual typewriter, so when she joined the computer-savvy *Emigre* and was given a high-end Apple Macintosh to use, she was new to the technology—but eager to learn.

Even with a typeface under her belt and her newfound computer literacy, Liz still didn't really think of herself as a technology worker. With her liberal arts major she just didn't imagine herself as destined to follow a technology path. She was actually working as a freelance writer when she wrote some marketing pieces for Apple about the Newton (an early handheld Personal Digital Assistant [PDA]) and started using QuarkXPress to do layout work for her own projects. She designed her own business cards and even designed custom FiloFax pages when she decided she didn't like the typeface that came with the DayRunner she used.

Being a freelance writer had its advantages, but Liz had expected it to be a much more inspiring endeavor than it actually turned out to be. She found that she was rarely able to write anything creative and, more often than not, had to write mundane pieces for picky editors who were really more interested in how concisely she could relay the content than in her writing style. So since she'd heard about all the cool projects being generated in the technology field and happened to be conveniently located close to Silicon Valley, she decided to try her hand at writing for technology companies.

In 1994, when she landed a job as a technical writer for General Magic, a spin-off of Apple, Liz finally considered herself part of the world of technology. At General Magic, Liz was asked to write a manual documenting how to create a ROM chip for hardware manufacturers that were building devices using General Magic's operating system. She had only a minimal grasp of what she was supposed to be documenting and set to work reading every available document on General Magic's intranet so that she could figure out all the technical terms she needed to understand. She then augmented that learning by reading programming manuals, searching out the company engineers to help her fill in the gaps, and even tapping into a community of technical writers from outside the company who could help her if there were parts of the manual she couldn't figure out. Her "no fear" approach to asking questions helped her succeed.

Later some of Liz's co-workers at General Magic left to work at WebCrawler, a popular Internet search engine at the time. They hired her to join them there and then, and in a flurry of the ever-popular acquisitions that are part of the Web landscape, Excite bought WebCrawler and then @Home bought Excite. When the smoke cleared, Liz found herself working as the senior producer for the Shopping Channel at Excite@Home, where she helped to establish one of the Web's most successful networks, before deciding to delve into a new adventure with Spotlife.com.

Moving through the rash of acquisitions and being

exposed to life in Silicon Valley is an experience Liz is eager to share. She's writing a novel about power dynamics, money, and the emergence of a new type of "alpha male" in Silicon Valley, and is enjoying committing the things she sees in the Valley to paper. "It's a general Silicon Valley snapshot of life," she says. "I've been working in the Valley for five years now and I've gotten to know a lot of real characters and interesting stories."

Typeface
A typeface is the ornamental manifestation of the alphabet. If the alphabet conveys words, a typeface conveys their tone, style, and attitude.

We can all look forward to Liz's telling of Valley goings-on, such as the long-running prank in which engineers pop open each other's computers and put hardboiled eggs and hot dogs next to the motherboards. Only months later when the foods starts to emit all kinds of unwelcome odors is the prank discovered.

Yes, to hear Liz tell it, life in the Valley isn't quite as glamorous as the newspapers and magazines would have us believe. It's full of the same low-brow humor found everywhere else, and, thanks to Liz Dunn, it's coming soon to a bookstore near you.

Zuzana Licko
Emigre Fonts
www.emigre.com

Mrs Eaves is an historical revival based on the design of Baskerville, a classic design from the letter press era. (It is named after Sarah Eaves, who became John Baskerville's wife after the death of her first husband.)

 In translating this classic to today's digital font technology, I focused on capturing the warmth and softness of letter press printing that often occurs due to the "gain" of impression and ink spread. The second phase of this typeface development was designing a collection of fanciful ligatures (connected letter pair designs) which emulate the contextual attention to detail of hand lettering.

Mrs Eaves

THE AARDVARK GOGGLES

Deconstructivist theorists be freeky

SUPER AMBIENT LAVA LAMP

Affinity with happy gift sprees

Emily Ann Field

Lead Interactive /ITV Producer
MSNBC Interactive
www.msnbc.com

When she was growing up, Emily Field wanted to be Jane Pauley. Today Emily is a lead interactive producer with **MSNBC.com**, and while Emily Field may not be a household name, much of what she does behind the scenes is helping to revolutionize reporting and broadcasting as we know it.

With her sights set on a career as a television reporter, Emily studied journalism at Boston University. She was working toward a career in traditional reporting when she got sidetracked by new media. Boston University was offering a new-media program that sounded intriguing, and so she signed up. This led to a job writing and editing a guidebook to CD-ROMs in 1994, which quickly cemented her interest in digital storytelling and convinced her that

working on the Internet would be more fun and more creative than a traditional television reporting job.

At age 25, Emily is already a key manager at MSNBC Interactive. She leads a staff of interactive producers who are responsible for both long-term and daily "interactives," applications that are built to complement stories on the

MSNBC Web site. Working with these producers, Emily is responsible for bringing online and television news together in a daily news cycle. This means everything from researching statistics to writing JavaScript code.

Emily also oversees the staff of the Interactive Television (ITV) department. MSNBC.com produces interactive television broadcasts of NBC's *Nightly News,* the *Today Show* and *Dateline* NBC for the WebTV-plus platform. The ITV producers work to prepare these broadcasts by adding features, including in-depth editorial, stock quote look-ups, community chats, weather information, and personalized health quizzes.

All this responsibility has been earned through hard work, constant creativity, and a commitment to learning. Ten-hour days are part of the deal, and even once Emily gets home in the evening, she is constantly checking email and news feeds from her fully wired home office. Here's what a day in the life of Emily Field might include:

9:30 Attends a "budget call" where the Lead News producers discuss and determine the top news stories and priorities for the day.

10:00 Coordinates daily requests and story ideas with her team, scheduling in time for longer feature packages.

10:30 Spends the rest of the morning covering news, watching wire services for updates, and looking for interactive possibilities. Emily is constantly coordinating with whatever programming NBC News is planning for its OnAir shows.

12:00 Budget call that incorporates all the sections of the MSNBC.com Web site. Priorities for the afternoon are established at this meeting.

12:30 Emily is responsible for making sure that her team hits their news deadlines—as well as for staying on top of software delivery schedules for applications her team may be programming outside the news cycle.

3:00 Concentrates on preparing programming for NBC's *Nightly News*, *Dateline*, and the next morning's *Today Show*.

5:00 Final news budget.

6:00 Watches and monitors the Eastern time zone broadcast of NBC's *Nightly News*.

Throughout the day, Emily is also attending design reviews and planning meetings. She works frequently with marketing and advertising sales staff, attends code reviews, and conducts usability tests on new applications being prepared for broadcast.

Emily is working at the forefront of the convergence of television and the Internet. She's demonstrating her leadership abilities on a day-to-day basis and learning to be comfortable as a young woman in an industry that has traditionally been dominated by older, male managers.

> "If I'm not driving, eating, or sleeping, there's a computer running my email somewhere near me."

Emily includes her mother, Madeleine Albright, and Jane Pauley among her mentors, and surely those women would be proud of the bright, confident woman they have influenced. They would share her commitment to overcoming gender stereotypes by believing in yourself and your ideas, and trusting your own instincts. And they would agree that new-media careers help to defeat gender and age bias by giving opportunities to people willing to be innovative, radical, and daring.

Emily Ann Field is all of those things. She's taking risks, daring to lead, and practicing innovation every day. She isn't a household name yet, but as news broadcasting changes, it may not be long before Emily steps into Jane Pauley's shoes and brings us the media-convergent news of the future.

Candis Callison

Senior Producer
Lycos Network
www.lycos.com

Candis Callison is a long way from home. Of all the technologies she hopes will be invented in the future, she lists
teleporting (*Star Trek* style) as the one she'd most like to
have available. "Beam me up" technology would make it
possible for Candis to visit her family without traveling
across a continent to get to the remote community where
she grew up.

Candis is a member of the Tahltan Nation. Her father was
born and raised in and around the Native communities of
Telegraph Creek, Dease Lake, and Iskut in northern British
Columbia. To travel to Telegraph Creek from Boston where
she lives now is a six-hour plane trip to Vancouver
followed by another two-hour flight to Whitehorse in the
Yukon. From there, it is a nine-hour drive to reach her

dad's house. This is as remote as
it gets and so it's understandable
that when Candis first told her
dad about her plan to leave
British Columbia, his first
thought was earthquakes, not
stock options or Silicon Valley.

And she's a long way from
home in other ways as well.
Since reaching adulthood, Candis
has tried to go home every

summer to spend time at her family's traditional hunting and fishing areas. There she spends time with her aunts, uncles, grandparents, and sisters. She fishes and goes to potlatches and feasts, and listens to her friends drumming and singing. In 1997, Candis and her husband, who's a member of the N'laka'pmx Nation, got married in "fish camp" about six miles outside Telegraph Creek.

Candis doesn't get many opportunities to attend potlatches these days. Now she buys her smoked salmon ready to eat instead of catching and smoking it herself. It's easy to understand how far away from the familiarity and camaraderie of her community she must feel sometimes.

She and her husband will go back to British Columbia one day, but for now she's decided to live wherever her passion for technology and commitment to building a rewarding career take her. Already her journey has taken her from filmmaking to television to the Web, where she is now putting her talents to work as a senior producer at Lycos.

The Lycos Network is one of the largest hubs on the Internet. Its network of sites provides Web search and navigation services as well as communication and personalization tools, home-page building, and a shopping center. At Lycos, Candis manages and produces a Web Guide that aggregates content from third-party providers. This is a challenging job that has little precedent. To do it well you need to be able to multitask and work well with many different groups simultaneously to bring together a cohesive product every day.

Candis's daily meetings with engineering, development, quality assurance, and design teams help her to stay on top of what's happening on any given day. She also works regularly with product management and business development to make deals and get new content partnerships under way for the Web Guide. She works with the Usability Lab and Design

Team to make sure she's meeting the needs of her users as well. All told, her job is one that requires her to work quickly, effectively, and openly with almost everyone at the company. This means having excellent management and creative skills, things Candis

> "There are as many women with a predisposition for math, science and technology, as there are for housecleaning, administration, and real estate."

honed during her early days in the television industry.

She entered the television industry after doing some work on a documentary series for B.C. Hydro. She became a regular contractor at CBC television, and even started her own production company, where she made her first broadcast documentary. Always looking for new challenges, Candis moonlighted in the Aboriginal community, working as everything from a comic book writer to a producer of not-for-broadcast television programming. While she continued to build her experience in traditional media, Candis became increasingly interested in technology and new media. She was using the Internet regularly for research and found herself explaining technology to those around her. While working as a producer and series cohost at Vancouver Television, she discovered an opportunity to put all that knowledge into action. She launched a Web site for Vancouver Television and developed their first technology report for television news. In the process she became fascinated with the marriage of television and the Internet, and started looking for new ways to expand her horizons.

With this in mind, in 1998, Candis accepted an offer to work with ZDTV, the first cable network devoted to computers and technology, based in San Francisco, California. There she worked as a reporter and producer for *The Money Machine*, reporting on e-commerce and financial news for a national U.S. audience.

From ZDTV Candis came to her current position at Lycos,

a company that allows her to bring her talents and interests to a fast-paced environment that keeps her challenged and engaged. "I think I bring a lot to the table as someone who has amassed experience in both traditional and new media," Candis says. And she's right. Her background is still a rarity in new media, even as we see more and more convergence between traditional media and the Internet. Her ability to work on tight budgets and time lines, as well as her "Okay, we're live and on the air" attitude, serves her well at Lycos and will continue to be great assets as she charts new Internet territory.

Susan Sowah

Senior Account Executive
Cebra, Inc.
www.cebra.com

Susan Sowah learned about computers the way a lot of women learn about computers—from her children. In 1989, Susan's five children were all under the age of 12 and were starting to use computers at school. They were excited about computing, were trading computer games with other kids in the neighborhood, and were begging Susan to get them a PC to use at home. Susan realized that if she wanted to figure out what her kids were up to, she should invest some time learning about computers and understanding technology.

Learning about computers wasn't the only life-altering event headed Susan's way in 1989. On Valentine's Day the same year, after marrying young and being a mom for over a decade, Susan woke up and told her husband she wanted

a divorce. She'd spent all week searching the store aisles for a Valentine card that might express a sentiment she actually felt, and had come up empty-handed. "If Hallmark has nothing to say to your relationship, you should get the hell out," Susan quips with a half smile.

Whatever the reason, Susan knew the relationship was over

and was determined to make a new start. This confident woman, now the embodiment of ease, wisdom, and humor, can happily and even proudly recount a morning that, at the time, must have been terrifying. Still only 31 years old, Susan was suddenly a single mom with five young children relying on her. It was clear that her part-time job at the local school board wasn't enough, so one of the first things on Susan's agenda was to search for work.

She set out to make a list of the qualities she was looking for in permanent employment. In her candid, forthright way she remembers that her list was one born of practicality. In order to juggle motherhood with a career, Susan knew she would need flexible hours and big-time money.

She says that no heavy lifting and a chance to travel topped her criteria. With these qualities laid out, Susan knew immediately that only a few career paths could satisfy her needs. "The short list came down to 'heiress' and 'sales,'" Susan says, "and so I was cornered into a sales job which turned out to be the hardest, most underpaid work I'd ever done."

But she persevered and things improved. Her first job in technology really wasn't in technology at all, but at least the company had the word computer in its name, which, to a good salesperson like Susan, was enough. She had landed a job selling computer diskettes, computer paper, and printer ribbons for a commercial sales operation. She was on her way, and credits a generous man named Bruce Jaffries for making a recommendation to management and giving her this much-needed shot at success.

Today, just a decade later, Susan is the senior account executive for Cebra, Inc., a member of the Bank of Montreal group of companies that focuses on e-commerce initiatives. She's currently working on a joint venture between Cebra and Canada Post called EPOST, a Web-based solution that provides complete electronic mail delivery services, including bill presentment and payment, statements, correspondence, and electronic forms.

Susan's role within EPOST is to be responsible for the corporate acceptance and sales of the venture. She spends her days either in front of a customer, preparing to be in front of a customer, or following up on a meeting with a customer. She is entirely customer focused and so, although her product would not be possible without technology, the technology is not the center of her world. Susan believes that the EPOST solution must provide for improvements in other areas (i.e., costs, customer satisfaction, receivables, customer support); otherwise, there is no reason for anyone to buy it. In her familiar refrain, Susan points out, "it isn't about the technology—it's about improving how we do things."

You hear this idea from Susan again and again when you talk to her. Amid the stream of positive energy that pours from her is a message she wants to share: technology is not a self-contained skill set that you either have or you don't.

According to Susan, technology is actually the easiest part of her job. "Pure technology is nothing more than a specific kind of information that can

---

Every line of work has its own jargon or secret code to keep out the non-practitioners. Often, in technology, the jargon is in the form of a TLA, or "three-letter acronym." There is even an acronym TWAIN, which stands for Technology Without An Interesting Name. Recently, two colleagues were discussing how FINs had really interesting technology. Not wanting to look like I wasn't "in-the-know," I started running through my mental Rolodex, thinking "Financial," "Floating," "Information," "Integer," "Node," "Number" . . . Finally I broke down and asked, "Who are FINs?"

My two friends fell silent and stared at me blank-faced for a second.

"People from Finland," they told me.

> I have the same relationship with my computer and my car. They are both vehicles that allow me to travel, escape, and explore, and that offer me the freedom to conduct my life in the way I choose. I am not particularly interested in the inner workings of either. Should either one break down, I want a professional to quickly get the machinery up and running with the least amount of inconvenience to me and without boring me with the gory details of what was actually wrong with it. I am not interested in mechanics—I am interested in the travel.

be acquired with diligent study and commitment," she says. Things such as customer management, sales, and negotiation are the real skills that, when combined with a knowledge of technology, can make you great at your job.

This is something a lot of us forget. When women, especially older women, from outside the industry meet Susan, they often remark that she must be really "technical." It's the technical part of what she does that people focus on and that often scares people away from learning more. This just reinforces her concerns over how technology is misunderstood and who is implementing the technology. "When Plato defined the types of people required to build and contribute to a city, he didn't just name architects and politicians," Susan reminds us. "In the *Republic*, Plato told us that cities also require hairdressers, teachers, farmers, and seamstresses. Similarly, in today's information age, we must recognize that our cities will continue to benefit from the collective genius of all of us, or they will be less than they might have been."

culture

introduction

A ship in port is safe, but that is not what ships are for.
Sail out to sea and do new things.

—Admiral Grace Hopper,
computer pioneer

Charting a course into the world of technology can be a
daunting challenge for women. Today's computer culture is
still dominated by men, and many women have yet to navigate these largely uncharted waters. New technologies
have become increasingly important and arguably necessary in some spheres of modern life. In light of this sea of
change, it becomes imperative for women to heed the
words of Admiral Hopper and set sail into new territory.

Yet, computer culture was not always a male domain. In
fact, some of the first computer researchers, programmers,
and experts were women. While completing graduate studies at Harvard University and MIT, I began to explore the
world of gender, technology, and computer culture. To my
surprise, I uncovered the stories of Ada Byron Lovelace,
Admiral Grace Murray Hopper and the ENIAC women.
Lovelace was a brilliant mathematician who helped to intro-
duce a computer binary system and set the groundwork for
much of the work of programmers later to come. Similarly,
Hopper was instrumental in the early development of
computer assembler language. In 1945, six young women,
Marlyn Meltzer, Ruth Teitelbaum, Kay Antonelli, Frances
Spence, Jean Bartik, and Betty Holberton, programmed a
machine called the Electronic Numerical Integrator and
Computer (ENIAC) and were instrumental in changing the
face of computer programming.

Excited as I was to discover these hidden stories, I was

disappointed to realize that the efforts of these and other pioneering women remained largely unrecognized. For the last few hundred centuries, women have put their energy into reclaiming their voices, experience, and presence in all facets of history, and I was dismayed to think that these contributions to technology might remain unacknowledged. To this end, we have worked together to bring you the stories of today's brave women as they continue to venture into the virtual high seas of technology.

In this section of the book you'll discover the women who are educators, artists, musicians, and intellects—strong voices emerging from diverse backgrounds and experience to come together in a collective voice of culture. These stories speak to each other, and part of the pleasure of reading them is discovering that dialogue. Many of these women have asked each other and themselves important questions about identity, gender, esthetic, and culture and have each explored how these topics intersect with technology.

I hope you enjoy these stories as much as we have. Together may we continue to explore the exciting world of technology and embark on new voyages of discovery.

Denise Shortt

Sherry Turkle
"Cyber Sociologist"
http://web.mit.edu/sturkle/www/

Sherry Turkle is one of the world's leading thinkers on gender, technology, and computer culture. You may know her face: Sherry is professor of Sociology of Science at MIT and author of *Life on the Screen*, a book that examines the changing impact of the computer on our psychological lives, and she was the first woman to grace the cover of *Wired* magazine. In 1997 she was asked to chair a commission for the American Association of University Women on gender and technology. Sherry's groundbreaking research takes us "under the hood" with an examination of why some of us fear the machine. Her cutting-edge cultural analyses, insights, and knowledge of computers and communications make accessible to readers the story of how our relationship to computers is changing our minds and our hearts.

"Look, Mommy, a jellyfish—it looks so realistic." It's 1998, and Sherry Turkle and her seven-year-old daughter, Rebecca, are standing on the shore of the exquisitely blue Mediterranean Sea. Mother and daughter are supposed to be on holiday, but when Rebecca sees a live jellyfish and assumes it's a toy, the researcher in Sherry can't help but analyze her daughter's reaction. Fast-forward to the present and Sherry pairs this story with a conversation she had with a Disney executive. "He says, 'Well, you know, when they built Animal Kingdom'—which is a Disney theme park that is based on real animals, real biological animals—'visitors to the park complained that they weren't realistic enough because they were comparing them to the robotic, or rather animatronic I think they call it, crocodiles across the street in Disney World. And the robot crocodile behaves much more like essence of crocodile—it rolls its eyes, it slaps its tail. It even performs like essence of crocodile, whereas the real crocodile's basic attitude is, 'Listen, you brought me here. I'm lying in the mud.'"

The story of the crocodile and the jellyfish perfectly illustrate Dr. Turkle's latest interest in studying the culture of simulation, and her belief that the boundaries of the virtual and the real are becoming blurred for an entire new generation of children. Since all good research begins with a question, Sherry is quick to point out that the relevant one here is "What is the gold standard?" In other words, as we increasingly become exposed to simulated versions of reality, what will be the new standard of expectation for what "real" looks like? And as our children grow up within this heavily simulated culture, how will their notions of what is "real" and what is "virtual" be affected?

Fascinated by the human mind and psychology, Sherry Turkle has made a career out of tapping into our technological imaginations. How exactly are our "virtual" and "real" worlds overlapping? Can the virtual world improve real life? Is it possible to have a relationship with a computer? Will humans physically merge with technology to transform us into the "cyborgs" we've glimpsed in sci-fi films and novels?

Since her arrival at MIT in the late seventies, Sherry has cultivated her cyber curiosity and encouraged her colleagues and students to tackle these and other mind-tickling questions. For example, one of the professor's popular courses, called Gender, Technology, and Computer Culture, invites students from both MIT and Harvard University to examine how computers have changed the way people interact with the world and the way we view ourselves.

As you would expect, outside the classroom, Sherry is quite concerned about the general low level of public discourse on the topic of computers and computer culture. According to Sherry, our current conversations about technology seem to be mostly motivated by concern. For example, a societal focus on unhealthy conditions such as computer addiction may be clouding our collective understanding of our own fears about technology and blocking what we can really learn from our online relationships. In a recent interview, Sherry explained, "I think that many of our anxieties about the Internet are a displacement of other anxieties about the power of technology in our lives. People feel that computers are getting out of control, and they fear they can do nothing about it. Then they seize on the Internet and imagine that this is a place where they can exert control. So, they focus on censorship, on pornography, on filters."

Instead, Sherry urges us to open up our imagination to all of the fascinating possibilities that technological innovation has to offer, and warns us not to "close down all the interesting questions about how some people use the computer to really enhance their growth, their identities, their possibilities, their ability to change their lives."

To keep the dialogue on track, Sherry is doing her part by forming the Center for Technological Identity at MIT. Her goal is to create a think tank of diverse psychologists, developmentalists, psychiatrists, and humanists to study these sorts of psychological and sociological issues. "So, I see myself now as trying to build up, not just in my own writing and research, but through the creation of an institutional base, more sensitivity to these issues." Sherry believes that the current computer culture demands this kind of awareness, and that her contribution will be to create an environment where possibility prevails over phobia. Determined to extend this essential dialogue outside the hallowed halls of the Boston-based academic institution, she also intends to speak out more publicly, and invites all of us to raise the level of sophistication in our public discourse concerning computer technology.

As a licensed clinical psychologist, the 51-year-old professor's psychological schooling became the breeding ground for what she now sees as the job at hand: "to put the computer in its rightful place intellectually and emotionally." A graduate of Radcliffe College, Sherry went on to receive a joint doctorate in Sociology and Personality Psychology from Harvard University in 1976, and has since authored three books and numerous articles on our psychological culture, our computer culture, and on how the two have grown together. Her specialty is thinking about the computer as a psychological machine rather than merely as a business tool programmed to coldly calculate. After careful observation of countless computer users, Sherry continues to pose the questions, and reminds us that "the point is not just to be involved with technology; the point is—technology for what? What is it doing to us?"

Often referred to as the "Margaret Mead of cyberspace" and an online ethnologist, Sherry Turkle has devoted more than 20 years to the study of the relationship between humans and computer culture. Her groundbreaking work has helped reveal that computers are "forcing us to reflect on what we are, how we are like and not like the computer." In other words, Sherry believes our interactions with the computer can help us to better understand and even influence our own identity.

The notion that we make our technologies, but then our technologies in turn make and shape us, was at the forefront of Sherry's mind when she wrote her two influential books on computers and people. Her first book, *Psychoanalytic Politics: Jacques Lacan and Freud's French Revolution*, discussed how psychoanalytic ideas spread through popular culture. Sherry picked up this theme in her studies of computers and culture, investigating how computational metaphors influence the way people were coming to think about their minds. Her next book, *The Second Self: Computers and the Human Spirit*, was published in 1984, and in it Sherry analyzes the relationship between people and the machine. But by the late 1980s, computers had advanced into complicated communication devices, and this change encouraged Sherry to shift the focus of her research. Our relationship to computers is no longer exclusively "one-on-one with the machine," she says; in fact, with the advent of email and the Internet, we began to interact with other people "through the machine."

As the computer moved from being a device used only for business and science to one used for "profoundly personal purposes," Sherry acknowledged the Internet as an evocative psychological object. "I feel totally privileged. I mean, not just that I live in interesting times, but to have seen this technology develop from the point that it did, to be where it is now, and to try to be some kind of voice for looking at the subjective side of technology. And I have this distinction that I have made for such a long time, between the instrumental computer and the subjective computer—the computer that does things *for* us, and the computer that does things *to* us, as people. I think it has been very exciting for me to be a voice for that subjective computer, which I think can so often get lost in the shuffle."

Armed with the challenging task of acting as technological translator, Sherry turned her keen observational expertise toward those who experimented on the Net and played with their identity online. The Internet afforded new opportunities to form virtual communities, engage in online chat, or even role-play as the opposite sex or as a nonhuman entity, and Sherry was determined to find out what this kind of identity play does to the quality of our relationships and how it affects our "ROL" or "rest of life." "People use the Net to interact, act out, socialize, and effect change in their lives and identity. When people are online they can express different aspects of themselves . . . they have the option to do and say anything they want."

By the time she published her landmark third book in 1995, Sherry had discovered that the computer and the Internet had created a new space for psychological growth and discovery. In *Life on the Screen*, Sherry was one of the first proponents of the idea that identity on the Internet is fluid. In fact, for many online users, the Internet provides an opportunity to move fairly seamlessly back and forth between virtual and physical. Through Sherry's insight, we learned that reality for some had become just one more "window on the screen."

Suddenly, the Internet offered a new space for everything from digital fantasies to virtual affairs, and everyone wanted a peek. Tracking one technological trend to the next, Sherry refers to these early Internet years as a "time of intense experimentation." Touted as the world's leading "cyber-shrink," she was suddenly propelled into the popular media as an expert observer on topics ranging from cybersex to psychotherapy in cyberspace. In a 1996 cover story called "Sex, Lies and Avatars," *Wired* magazine called Sherry's second book "the first serious look at the multiple personalities we live in cyberspace." Clearly, the digital age had delivered a new paradigm of unique psychological case studies, but Sherry maintains that most kinds of online identity play are positive and even allow us to exercise a new flexibility and freedom from the "work-oriented nature of modern life."

Five years after the publication of *Life on the Screen*, the single mother has moved on to research topics that hit somewhat closer to home. Now, Sherry is busy examining the influx of virtual pets and digital dolls that have become the psychological playmates for a new generation of children. Her current research subject is the "Furby," a friendly, fuzzy, and unpredictable computerized doll that "talks, sleeps, blinks, and even asks to be fed." Sherry's preliminary research on kids and their day-to-day experiences with technological toys is telling. "What is very obvious is that children want to be successful with the Furby, not to win over it, but rather to establish a kind of relationship of mutual recognition. In other words, their fantasy is just being loved by the Furby, and they are loving it in return. The Furby then represents the tip of the iceberg, but the tip of the iceberg of a kind of technology that asks you to relate to it and understand it."

Sherry is hot on the trail of these brand-new "psychological machines," and she is particularly interested in exploring how these objects are invested with needs and emotions that ask us to relate to them the way you would to a person. Although she admits that most adults still find the idea of a machine with a consciousness deeply disturbing, she reminds us that the relational potential of these technological toys has already reached the marketplace. "Mitsubishi has introduced a pet robot cat to be a companion for older people. Sony has introduced a pet dog. Clearly, the whole pet metaphor is the way in which objects have increased in complexity and seduction. I think we need to reflect on what this means, and particularly for kids as they grow up, to have this whole new world of objects to relate to." Once again, the researcher in Sherry

takes time out to frame the appropriate set of questions.
"First of all, the question is, How do we conceptualize
these new relationships with objects? And then the second
question is, What kinds of relationships is it appropriate to
have with objects?"

The renowned expert on relationship research also recognizes the importance of how women relate to technology
and how some women's reactions to "the machine" have
undergone remarkable changes. Sherry tells the story of a
movement from phobia to friendship with the computer.
"Well, I am encouraged, in some ways, by the fact that for
years people talked about women and computer phobia, as
though they had a disease. And, in fact, this disease seemed
to have been cured to some remarkable degree, when
America Online became easy enough to really just plug in
to and women discovered, 'Wow, this technology is a
communications technology: I can be in touch with my
children; I can be in touch with my family. I can learn
about things I want to learn about. I can join communities,
like iVillage [**www.ivillage.com**], where I am getting information and connections that are crucial to me.' As a larger
number of women flock online and realized the computer
could be a tool that is powerful and helpful, the good news
story meant that the 'computer phobia is dying.'"

But Sherry has long since recognized how critical it is for
women to become more than just consumers of technology, and instead insists that it is imperative for us also to
be producers and designers of technology. "I think that
women are needed in the making and reshaping of this
culture and I think that the more empowered women feel
with it, the better." An early proponent of the idea that
women have the capacity to "remake the culture around the
machine," Sherry adds that "as the computer becomes more
and more a communications medium, and a medium on
which, on the Internet, you need to build consensus, you

need to build community—it is about communications, I mean, all of these 'C' words—that women are becoming more involved, and more central, in the development of the computer culture."

Although a female-inspired computer culture revolution appears to be under way, Sherry is on a mission to ensure that all girls have a fighting chance to boldly go where few women have gone before. Recently commissioned by the AAUW (American Association of University Women), she is leading a team of 14 professional researchers, educators, journalists, and entrepreneurs to study technology, gender, and teacher education. The newly formed think tank recently released a report entitled "Tech-Savvy: Educating Girls in the New Computer Age" that confirms Sherry's own belief that girls are not computer phobic but merely "reticent" about the importance and relevance of computers and technology in their lives. Sherry says, "I always preferred the term 'reticent' because reticence had to do with feeling that the technology was not addressing their needs, that they weren't getting something out of it . . . it wasn't about fear."

Nevertheless, the report does take girls' criticism of the computer seriously and supports the notion that our computer culture must be remade to meet the needs of girls and boys. To this end, Sherry and her colleagues introduced a series of recommendations that should encourage computer fluency in girls beyond using email. By inciting young imaginations, Sherry and her team believe we can inspire a new generation of girls to become lifelong learners and shapers of technology.

From examining psychological machines to empowering women and girls to re-make computer culture, Sherry Turkle has had a cutting-edge influence. In the new millennium, many more are realizing the critical value of Sherry's contributions. Small wonder, then, that she has been identified by many industry leaders as someone destined to lead us into our digital future. In 1995, *Newsweek* magazine named her in its "50 for the Future: the Most Influential People to Watch in Cyberspace." By 1997, *Time Digital Magazine* had put her on its list of the top "50 Cyber Elite," and countless other media outlets look to her for unique psychological perspective and guidance. It is clear that Sherry Turkle's work is convincing many of us to look more closely at our evolving relationship with computers and to ask some crucial questions.

Tessa Sproule

New-Media Journalist
Senior Online Producer/Editor, *Infoculture*
Cocreator, The Great Canadian Story Engine
www.storyengine.ca

"If I were given the power to . . . create a major news media organization from the ground up, I'd start by centralizing the newsrooms into one place," says Tessa Sproule. "I'd gather the assignment editors, producers, and reporters into one place, and coordinate coverage and assign stories to the best reporters and producers to spin the items for radio/TV/print and the Web."

She may have just described the newsroom of the future, but today, Tessa sits in the newsroom of the past—a fabric-walled, tiny cubicle bunkered in a national broadcasting station. She's at the beginning of her professional climb: no big desk, no underlings; no office with a view. Her window on the world is her computer screen.

Tessa is simultaneously creating, covering, and riding a wave of change in, the world of communications. Her career reveals how our media world is shifting, and how one person can influence its evolution as old technologies and new converge.

As producer and editor of *Info-culture*, the online arts and culture magazine of the Canadian Broadcasting Corporation (CBC), she's responsible for many management aspects of the Web site—from hiring and firing, to securing a budget and pleading for its increase. She's responsible for thinking of special projects ("such as our live Webcast from the premiere of *Star Wars*"). "And a large, but hard to measure, part of my job is envisioning where we should be headed and making sure the site staff have that goal in focus too."

As a member of the CBC's new-media board, a primary area of responsibility is increasing *Infoculture*'s co-productions with existing radio and TV programs produced by the national broadcaster.

How did someone with no practical newsroom experience end up in this position? During her last year in journalism school, Tessa landed a job as writer/director for a national network radio program. By the time she graduated, she was working full-time as a producer. Assigned to cover the opening of "MediaLinx h@bitat," the Canadian Film Centre's new media training center founded by filmmaker Norman Jewison, she was so impressed by what she saw there that she quit her job and enrolled in the school's inaugural class.

Before she'd finished at h@bitat, the CBC had hired her back to help build and run an online arts and entertainment magazine. That site (*Infoculture*) is now one of the national network's fastest growing Web sites and a popular destination for anyone on the Web looking for rich and practical content about Canada's arts scene.

Tessa says reporters and producers who think they're multitasking big-time today are in for a shock. "Reporters and producers in the future will have to anticipate that their stories might end up in radio, print, TV, or Web form," she predicts. "It might be played, read, or heard by the audience in a familiar form—say, radio—or in something we've yet to invent. Have you seen those tablet PCs?"

Reporters and producers will also have to come to terms with the fact that they're not objective, says Tessa. "Even today, the journalist is being pushed into the role of messenger—not filterer—of information. Technology allows the audience a window on the entire journalism process—from the ability to provide instant feedback (through email or discussion boards, i.e., instant Letters to the Editor), to the potentially enormous impact of being able to open up the reporter's notebook.

At *Infoculture*, when reporters write articles, they also post their research material and an unedited copy of their interviews to the site for the audience to peruse. The impact seems slight at first, but it has profound implications, says Tessa. "By listening to and reading the source of the story, the audience can see our bias . . . can see which portions of the interview were used and, more importantly, those which weren't . . . can hear the questions we asked—and didn't. The result, I hope, is more responsible media and a more aware audience."

Will new-media monoliths be equal-opportunity employers? Asked to name some new-media females who might serve as role models for young women, Tessa admits none immediately come to mind.

"I'm not sure if this is the fault of the media—for not showcasing the talent of women working in the industry—or if we should believe that all the interesting things being done in new media really are being done by men and men alone . . . But this is an exciting industry to be working in. We're paving the way for tomorrow—however clichéd that sounds, it's true. And that's remarkable. The opportunities are boundless, so long as you're willing to take some risks."

As a coproducer of the Great Canadian Story Engine (www.storyengine.ca), Tessa's out front on a major, national millennium project: to define one country's identity through personal storytelling. The "engine"—the first fully developed project to come out of MediaLinx h@bitat—consists of two parts: a "living engine," a digitally outfitted, mobile exhibit and classroom that tours Canada gathering stories from coast to coast, and a "virtual engine" or Web site that reflects the stories gathered on that tour. Essentially, it's an online repository of stories, a digital tapestry that weaves and links together the lives of Canadians from every walk of life.

The collective brainchild of Tessa and other h@bitat students—Kato Wake, Rand Ardell, Jason Cliff, and Rena Dempsey—the Great Canadian Story Engine was launched in spring 2000. Tessa hopes the Story Engine Web site will be filled with 2000 stories by fall 2000.

Sorcha Ni hEilidhe

Senior Editor of *Nua Internet Surveys*
www.nua.ie/surveys/

Sorcha Ni hEilidhe is "into" the Internet, partly because her cyber career allows her to make a name for herself in her field without having to be judged by her appearance. "The Internet allows you to be faceless. You can get a whole lot of leverage out of a name because people don't know if you're male or female, young or old. I am young. I'm fairly 'radical' looking, yet my readership thinks I am a 50-something Wall Street business lady with a suit and briefcase."

As senior editor of the Ireland-based Internet research publication *Nua Internet Surveys*, Sorcha's name is easily recognizable within the global IT community. Sorcha, 26, recently appeared live on a New York television show and the audience responded with incredulity. "The reaction of the majority of people to me was incredible. I am not what people expect."

So, why the surprised reaction to Sorcha? Here's how she describes herself:

Hair: plum-ish with streaks of infra red through it
Piercings: Belly button only
Tattoos: One on my left arm
Clothes: Street
Attitude: Big

Despite her unconventional appearance and ample attitude, Sorcha takes her role at the publication very seriously. "Nua is one of the most respected publications on the Net. I have to maintain the high standard of the publication. To give you an idea of what that means, the U.S. Department of Commerce recently quoted us. I have to be the authoritative voice on emerging trends. I have to speak to the press and account for my thinking."

Sorcha considers it a privilege to be paid "to ponder." "My job allows me to think about things. For example, the relationship between technology and society, the effects of the Internet on society and other such highfalutin concepts. I like my job because I'm paid to think about things I think about anyway."

Sorcha claims Nua has earned its place of respect within the competitive (whoever gets the most clicks wins) Internet industry by being rigorous, cutting edge, and responsive to the ever-changing economy. "Nua is the Irish [Gaelic] word meaning 'new.' It underpins the fundamental philosophy of Nua. We are in a new age, a digital age. A new age requires new thinking, a need to challenge traditional business models and management thinking. In this new age, people are paramount; they are empowered to challenge, to think, and to create new business principles to succeed in the digital age."

Sorcha also gives solid insight into the recent expansion of Ireland's economy, which is being hailed as an "economic miracle" and has earned the country the title Celtic Tiger. The republic's overall growth is due largely to its burgeoning hi-tech sector and investment from TransNational Corporations (TNCs) and Sorcha describes the positive impact of the foreign-inspired boon: "The Celtic Tiger owes a lot to these predominantly U.S. companies who have either set up shop in Ireland or bought local businesses. Rather than this being a cause for concern, it has reshaped the Irish economy and brought both much-needed financial capital and perhaps more importantly a real sense of entrepreneurialism into the country."

Sorcha adds that foreign competition will strengthen the industry and increase quality of

> **ISP:** An ISP (Internet Service Provider) is a company that provides connections to the Internet and access to Internet services such as email, the World Wide Web, and more recently, video and telephone services.
>
> An ISP may provide dial-up access or high speed access through broadband technologies such as the cable modem network or DSL (Digital Subscriber Line).

products and services for the all-important user of technology. "There are 3.5 million potential consumers in Ireland, and any company who chooses to ignore their needs will be superseded by a company who listens. The Internet puts purchasing power firmly in the hands of the consumer. Everything is a click away, and people are not afraid to exercise their mouse! I don't think that geography has anything to do with international markets in an online context."

Sorcha herself was not drawn to the Internet as a consumer, but rather as someone who was interested in the concept of the Internet as a new mass medium. "I was fascinated by its potential effect on society as opposed to being interested in the actual technology."

However, in her teens and early twenties, Sorcha didn't realize she was destined for a career in technology. Hence, her unconventional and somewhat eclectic career path, and her former quest to be either an environmental worker or a

WAN: A WAN (Wide Area Network) is a network that spans large geographical distances. The computers on a WAN may be located in different cities or even countries. In a WAN, some network communication goes through a third-party carrier network.

WAP: The WAP (Wireless Application Protocol) is a set of standard communications protocols that enable wireless devices, such as cell phones and PDAs, to access the Internet.

Emy Tseng

Software Engineer &
Researcher

MIT Internet & Telecoms
Convergence Consortium

rock star . . . whichever happened first. "I worked as an events organizer for Dublin AIDS Alliance for a year where I got to meet megastars like Bono and Naomi Campbell. I organized massive tribal gatherings and gave the proceeds to Earthwatch, an environmental organization. Worked as a promoter in the fledgling Irish music industry. Tried my hand as a spoken-word poetess, modeled on Lydia Lunch. Worked as a waitress. Busked around Europe. Traveled to Venezuela, Colombia, Trinidad, and Tobago with a camera, and wrote poetry. Umm . . . need I go on?"

But role models such as Esther Dyson ("I love the way she thinks") (see p. 67) helped steer Sorcha onto the technology trail, and she decided to put her Dublin City University communications degree to work. Now, along with her fellow Europeans, Sorcha strives to contribute to the global community of hi-tech. "I would say Europeans have just as much impact on the industry as North Americans. For example, Europe is the driver of WAP [Wireless Application Protocol] technology right now."

Amidst the world of WAPs, WANs, and ISPs, Sorcha is dedicated to keeping us informed of the increasing overload of acronym-labeled technological innovations as well as monitoring emerging digital trends. So, Sorcha, what else is NUA?

Grace Chung

PhD Candidate, MIT Laboratory of Computer Science
and Jazz Singer
www.gracechung.com

Grace Chung lives up to her first name. She is a graceful woman—a fascinating woman with a multitude of talents that seem to harmonize perfectly within her. She is an engineer, a mathematician, and a jazz singer.

After studying electrical engineering and mathematics at the University of New South Wales in Australia, Grace was accepted into a graduate program at the Massachusetts Institute of Technology. In addition to mastering life as a fifth-year graduate student, Grace works as a research assistant with the MIT Laboratory of Computer Science, Spoken Language Systems Group, developing speech-recognition technologies that will soon make it possible for our computers to respond to our voices as well as they do to fingers on a keyboard.

When she's not sitting at her computer, she's standing in front of a microphone, bringing her rich, soulful jazz stylings to audiences in Boston and New York. Grace performs with an all-female jazz ensemble called WhoSheBe. She cofounded WhoSheBe in 1998, and has found performing as a jazz vocalist to be a creative outlet that combines her spiritual and intellectual sides and gives her a chance to practice spontaneous improvisation as well as emotional expression. Her passion for performing and her love of the music make Grace an absolute pleasure to listen to and leave you marveling at the two seemingly distinct passions that fill her days and nights.

At first glance Grace's musical life does seem to be in stark contrast to her technology career. One is a public communication with an audience, while the other is private. Programming is an intellectual activity, while singing is a physical one. But both pursuits are born of Grace's creative strengths. In different ways they challenge and fulfill her and give her a chance to work with diverse groups of people to create works of art.

Perhaps one day she'll find a way to combine her two skills in a single project, but, for now, excelling at both makes Grace inspiring proof that whatever your passions, you can find a way to make your life a coming together of the things you love.

Angela DeMontigny

Spirit Ware Fashion Designer
http://spiritwarecanada.com

Talented young fashion designer Angela DeMontigny has little time left in the day to design clothes. Like most entrepreneurs, she is solely responsible for all aspects of her business, including the finances, daily operations, and even public relations. Angela, 36, says marketing and sales consume most of her energy and effort; that is, they did until the advent of the Internet. Now, the online tool has freed up her time and has proven to be an excellent catalyst for keeping her business creative, competitive, and connected.

Angela's Native-inspired clothing is especially popular in the U.S. Midwest and Southern California, and she needed to find a cost-effective method to reach her audience. Her Web site enables her to advertise her business globally without ever having to leave her home on the Six Nations

Mohawk reserve in Ontario.

The Internet is also crucial for spreading the cultural message behind her clothes. The Native influence and philosophy behind her fashions are crucial to the integrity of her designs and reputation: "We make people aware of the cultural aspects of our clothing. All items come with an explanation of the designs, which can range from influence by Iroquoian to Plains to Navajo." The entire Spirit Ware line is also designed and detailed by Native artisans. "Each tag gives an overview of the beadwork and the name of the person and/or their Nation or their Native name. These labels give the clothes a Native identity and lend authenticity to the item. It's important for this kind of information to reach our consumers."

So far, the biggest online challenge for Angela has been to register her site with all the major search engines using the proper key words and identifiers. She originally registered with what she assumed would be common-sense words appropriate for her business: Native fashion, design, clothing, etc. But it took her nearly two years to realize her market niche was actually "Western wear." "Who would've thought Native apparel would be sold under that category? I thought cowboys didn't like Indians," she laughs.

Angela also uses the Internet to monitor competitive sites, access resources of associations and affiliates, and keep up with the often frenetic fashion world. Isolated on the reserve, where she manufactures her clothing and operates her retail outlet, she relies on the Internet to keep her informed. She also works closely with her husband and partner, John, who is a graphic designer, artist, and computer wiz. Together they launched the Spirit Ware Web site and watched as queries and orders from as far away as Kuwait and Germany came flooding in.

Originally from British Columbia, Angela grew up not knowing much about her Native heritage. Her father believed his children would be better off if the family assimilated and tried to live "like normal Canadians." She was in her twenties when she finally fully embraced her Cree Métis origins and began to incorporate her ethnic legacy into her passion for fashion. Today, Spirit Ware sells "everywhere," and Angela says their success is due in part to the Internet, as sales over the past year have grown by 75 percent. The company was also recently commissioned to design clothing for the Canadian Aboriginal Awards, a ceremony that recognizes high achievement.

Angela says that she will continue to look for ways to use new technologies to help streamline her business and, by extension, promote her Native inheritance. She says, "Spirit Ware is a Native-owned and -operated company from the designer and production team to the administration staff. We are following the tradition of generations of artisans creating those specific designs and techniques handed down to them and utilizing them in a contemporary way. *Nya:weh/Meegwetch.* (Thank you.)"

Carolina Cruz Santiago

Executive Producer, channelP.com—The Performance Channel
Pseudo Programs, INC.
www.pseudo.com

Carolina Cruz Santiago feels incredibly lucky to have one of the most exciting jobs she's ever even heard of. Carolina is the executive producer of channelP, the arts and culture channel at **Pseudo.com**. Pseudo is a video-streaming network that broadcasts all kinds of creative programming over the Web and is one of the driving forces behind the increasing popularity of online broadcasting. As a producer at Pseudo, Carolina's roles range from developing content to managing production and developing new business.

After receiving a bachelor of science degree in design from the University of California at Davis, Carolina began a career in exhibition design, developing physical spaces where people could experience art by walking through her creations. But she grew tired of sitting at a drafting table for hours on end and decided she wanted to find some other ways to interact with art. She then worked with arts organizations, developing educational curricula and leading exhibit tours, before joining The Bay Consulting Group, an arts management consulting firm with clients such as the National Endowment for the Arts, the Pew Charitable Trusts, and the Knight Foundation.

Next Carolina began searching for new ways audiences could access the arts. She was intrigued with how technology was influencing the art world and decided to explore this aspect of the industry. After meeting a representative from Pseudo.com at a conference dedicated to technology and the arts, Carolina went on a studio tour, and a month later was assisting on the production of a poetry show. Within a couple of months she was brought on board as a producer, which then led to her current position as executive producer for channelP.

Carolina's interest in technology was sparked by the grassroots nature of the Web and the idea that so many different voices and opinions can now be shared in a forum that is open and accessible to people around the world. She saw streaming media and the Web as an extension of this new accessibility and as a way to bring her passion for the arts to a new medium and a new audience.

Carolina is also passionate about the opportunities for women that she sees in technology now. "With streaming media and the Internet," she says, "it's the wild, wild west." There are creative projects cropping up everywhere you look and tons of small businesses always looking for smart people with good ideas. Carolina has combined her own brains and good ideas with her willingness to work hard (13-hour days are par for the course, she says) to bring her incredible success early in her career.

But it hasn't been easy. Particularly now that she's working in television production (an industry traditionally dominated

Sometimes referred to as "rich media," **streaming media** is at once a technology and an umbrella term for online video-based entertainment. Essentially, streaming is a technique for transferring digital content whereby a server sends out a steady stream of 1s and 0s that are reassembled on the users' computer by a compatible software application. The result is a television-like experience for the user. Today, RealNetworks and Microsoft are streaming media's leading technology providers.

Joanne Marino
CEO / Editor-in-Chief
Webnoize

by men), she admits that being a woman can be difficult. She knows that sometimes she isn't taken as seriously as her male counterparts and often finds herself working twice as hard as they do in order to be recognized. This has been frustrating, of course, but she has chosen to combat this feeling by acknowledging that women often do still have to prove themselves in uncharted territory and by deciding it is up to her to do her part to change that reality.

Carolina might have imagined that she'd like to work on the other side of the camera, but her experience when one of her panelists didn't show up for a taping quickly changed her mind. Feeling confident that she knew the material, Carolina agreed to fill in for the missing panelist, only to have her mind go completely blank as soon as the red light went on. She couldn't remember what she wanted to say and everything that came out of her mouth was gobbledygook.

Having taken that experience as a sign that producing was the right role for her, after all, she went back behind the camera and started brainstorming about how best to bring arts programming to the Web. Carolina has experimented with a lot of roles already and is confident that being an executive producer is the ideal spot for her right now. Working behind the scenes to produce interactive arts programming allows her to balance organization and management with creativity and experimentation.

Carolina knew the arts community viewed technology differently than did many more traditional consumers, and was intrigued by the idea that artists would be open to finding creative uses for technology that weren't currently available. She realized she had an opportunity to serve the arts community with channelP, and today is excited to be part of the artistic evolution of the Internet. She enjoys contributing to the arts community's attempts to use technology to their advantage, specifically through the use of streaming media. At channelP, Carolina hopes that, slowly but surely, she's bringing arts programming to new audiences and having a positive impact on the way people access, experience, and think about art.

Janese Swanson
"A Virtual Room of Her Own"

Dr. Janese Swanson created her successful San Francisco–based company because her 10-year-old daughter would ask her questions such as, "Where are all the fun toys for girls?" Once she recognized the gap in girls' toys and software products, Janese did what many never do: she acted. The result was Girl Tech Inc., a company created to build toys and games that do more than just entertain. Girl Tech stuff is designed to strengthen the connection among girls through the use of technology. Its multi-award-winning Web site is one of the most popular playrooms for girls across North America, and the company's founder has been recognized for taking the women's revolution down the road into the new millennium. *Ms.* magazine nominated Janese "Woman of the Year" in 1997 and praised her as leading the charge in bringing girls into the world of technology.

Janese Swanson's secret to success stems from her refusal to listen to well-meant advice. Despite the glaringly apparent gender gap in the game, toy, and software industries, Janese received considerable resistance to her fresh concept for a girl-focused technology company. The message from industry experts and established software developers was consistent: "We don't make tech products for girls because boys won't buy them, whereas girls might buy tech products made for boys." Dubious financial advisors and venture capitalists denied Janese start-up funding not only because they felt they would be taking a huge risk by investing in technology just for girls, but because they were skeptical about the concept behind the company. Instead of developing just one technology product that would probably go unnoticed by the market, Janese had a bigger plan: to build an entire brand identity that would ultimately make a difference in the lives of girls worldwide. The bottom-line response from potential investors to this bold plan was a resounding "No!"

Nevertheless, the ambitious Janese turned a deaf ear to the so-called industry experts and chose to listen instead to questions posed by her daughter Jackie, such as, "Why aren't girls' toys cool, like boys' toys?" Taking this to heart, Janese forged ahead with her dream to encourage and empower girls in technology by creating products and services just for them.

As a respected veteran of the toy and software industry, Janese also relied on her own instincts and experience. She had already produced award-winning titles for Broderbund Software, including the hugely popular Where in the World is Carmen Sandiego? and the Playroom and Treehouse series. During her stint at Broderbund, Janese saw the company grow from a little family-run business into a giant international software developer, and this evolution fueled her own entrepreneurial drive. Soon after leaving Broderbund, Janese launched her first business venture called Kid One For Fun Inc., and she claims the company was "named for my number-one kid, Jackie, and because it was lots of fun." At Kid One For Fun, Janese designed clever electronic toys such as the "Yak-Bak," and cut her creative teeth within the competitive entertainment software business.

In 1995, Janese launched her new entrepreneurial initiative, Girl Tech Inc., but nothing could have prepared her for the struggle ahead. "We had no money—no money for three years. We were running our company on our credit cards and negotiating every step of the way. It was just total and pure grit to do this. And we were so determined, and I knew that it was the right thing to do, so I put it all on the line."

The Girl Tech founder and her core team of five dedicated women never doubted they were on the right track, but their struggle got worse before it got better. "As a woman, as a girl, and as somebody who was just bound and determined to get this accomplished, I had to do whatever it took. We are survivors, and in the beginning there really was just a handful of us who really had the spirit to keep this up." Despite the lack of industry support, Janese says she received nothing but encouragement from other women and her peers: "The concept of Girl Tech seemed so perfectly obvious, and desperately needed—an idea whose time had come. It just took a while to convince the industry."

Neither Janese nor her team had any formal computer science training, but they shared a strong belief in the way technology should be designed for girls. "I think that boys and girls should be treated equally with regards to technology; they should be encouraged equally, they should have an equal number of cool, fun, technology products designed for them; they should be expected to succeed in technology fields equally." Unfortunately, not one of those scenarios is the case today, so Janese is still set to level the playing field. She challenges anyone to pick up a gaming magazine, or go into any video arcade to truly see how male-dominated the industry is today. Janese admits girls are in a better place than a few years ago, but knows there is still a long way to go.

Faced with these daunting challenges, Janese and her team decided to launch their company on the Internet because it was cost-effective and the only place "we didn't get a 'no.'" In the early Internet years, there were no places on the Web for girls to find a community of peers and content that was created specifically for them. Now, thanks to Janese and her Club Girl Tech [www.girltech.com], there is such a place, with hundreds of pages of educational, entertaining, and inspirational content—from female role models to discussions about the genders, to technology product reviews. In 1997, Janese and her team also developed Tech Girl's Internet Adventure, a girl's guide to getting online along with a collection of popular Internet sites.

Girl Tech's first line of technological toys was produced with a seemingly simple goal: "to develop quality toys around proven play patterns." Their current series of electronic toys include the Password Journal, a girl's journal equipped with a voice-recognition locking device; Door Pass, which protects a girl's room with motion sensor and voice-recognition technology; Beam It, a projector that projects drawings and designs across a room; and Friend Frame, a programmable picture frame equipped with words other than "cute," "sweet," "pretty," and "nice." Some newer Girl Tech items slated to hit store shelves soon include a remote-control locking treasure box called the Keepsafe Box, and Bug 'em, a ladybug-shaped listening device. Based on solid research, surveys, focus groups, and feedback, Girl Tech has designed these products specifically to meet the needs of girls.

Janese Swanson and her company are committed to raising girls' awareness of and confidence in using technology, so as a single mom, she still looks to Jackie and other girls for input and inspiration in all phases of development. Janese's dedication to education and advocacy may also hearken back to her own girlhood passion for teaching. At age 20, Janese realized her dream of becoming a teacher, and claims she's been attending school ever since. So far, she has earned no less than seven college degrees in education, and by creating Girl Tech she has managed to find a way to take her penchant for learning in an entirely new direction.

The Girl Tech founder's greatest personal lesson, however, is to never give up on lifelong dreams even when the going gets tough. Now that Girl Tech's success is sound—due to their recent sale to Radica Games in 1998—Janese passes on some words of wisdom: "Listen to your heart and stay true to yourself. People change all the time, and that's okay. But if there's something in your heart that tells you that this is what you have to do, listen to yourself. Never let someone tell you 'no.' No matter how hard it gets, or how dark it gets, keep going, because if you don't give up, you'll win."

And that's the secret to success from one low-tech girl who, despite all odds, grew up to be a Girl Tech pioneer.

If You Were the Star of Your Own Video Game . . .

We asked some of the women we interviewed, "If you were the star of your own video game, what would your character look like and what would she do?" The answers we got were funny and creative—and thought-provoking as well.

She would look like Lara Croft but you'd hardly be able to see her because the dialogue boxes would be huge. She'd fight evil with carefully honed rhetoric.

—*Lynda Leonard*

She would be sexy, strong, and intelligent. She would be a lot like the character Dana Scully in *The X-Files* and would work with the player in trying to solve mysteries.

—*Sandra Smith*

She would be small with dreadlocks, and, as a student of Shaolin kung fu, she'd have crazy kung fu skills and thrills. She'd be kind of like Chun Li from the video game *Street Fighter*, but she would fight for truth, using her brain before brawn. She'd apply her study to all aspects of her life and would draw upon inner strength as opposed to physical, outer strength.

—*Nicole Blades & Natasha Kong*

"Snack Girl"—the superhero who saves the world from bad snacks like Combos and Smartfood. My weapons would be a Keebler cookie machine gun and invisible walls of Ben & Jerry's Ice Cream. My character would have an outfit made entirely of candy wrappers—a tank dress with a cape, and platform shoes, of course.

—*Carly Milne*

She would be "Tsipi the Humanitarian Warrior" (oxymoron? yes). The goal wouldn't be to kill the evil corporations who pollute or shoot the people who enslave children. Instead, it would be to figure out ways for people to come out ALIVE and WELL . . . it would be a game of solution not destruction.

—*Tsipora Mankovsky*

I think I've already subconsciously created her—my character would be "Womb." It would be a kid's role-playing game. The player could go around exploring Womb, climbing her walls, discovering key elements in the development of her fetus. When everything has been discovered at that level, the player could move on to the next stage of fetal development. There could be different modes—twin mode, triplet etc. . . . I'd buy it!

—*Bernadette Y. Lacarte*

A diva. My character would be an over-the-top, larger-than-life personality with brains. She would be mixed race, would speak multiple languages, would be some-what mysterious, and could never be outwitted.

—*Grace Chung*

She'd be built like Xena, but would wear a turtleneck every day and have James Bond–like eyeglasses with many, many purposes. By day, she'd be a video-journalist in a Max Headroom–type world where all her stories had an impact on societal problems. She'd also be able to transform herself into a hexidecimal-type character (nod to *Reboot* here) and fight evil inside machines.

—*Candis Callison*

Since it would be an adventure travel game, my video game character would be lean, athletic, and not too tall. She might have a ponytail that really swings. My character would have a gadget the size of a pen that can expand into equipment like a jet-powered snowboard for crossing the Himalayas while fleeing cyber-Sasquatches.

—*Sang Mah*

I've actually worked on this! "Agent All Black" is a superhero I modeled on a friend and made into a series of works about superheros. The names of the characters that emanated from the ether included "Trimalacious the Three-Headed Hostess Goddess," "Hitmaster," "Agent Little-Man," "Twig Boy & Agent Unvisible." It developed into an ongoing series of finger rockets named after airplane crashes.

—*Zina Kaye*

I'd be a supernatural superhero whose utterances would turn into throwing stars, tracking down evil consumer profilers and suppressors of free speech online. I'd look like a cross between Tank Girl, Lara Croft, and Michelle Yeoh. My kung fu would be deadly and I would be able to fly.

—*Tracy Smee*

She would be incredibly strong physically and emotionally, and most importantly she would be incredibly curious about everything (she could go online and learn a lot about anything!).

—*Farah Perelmuter*

She'd look like me. I love the game The Neverhood that, in the tradition of good old text-based games like Zork, was one of the first high-graphic games to rely entirely on story to propel the user to play. I would like my game to be highly immersive and not violent, with a main character who had to solve mind-numbing problems in a quest to save the world.

—*Tessa Sproule*

Maria Klawe
"Girl Games"

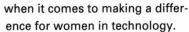

www.nserc.ca

As a woman who at one time had the desire to play Final Fantasy VII for her entire Christmas vacation, Maria Klawe knows only too well how obsessive many of us have become about computer games. The current Dean of Science at the University of British Columbia, she has spent years researching the computer play patterns of children, and she's come up with some remarkable results. Now she's committed to building educational and entertaining computer environments for children of both genders. She also wants to ensure that women are taking their rightful place as computer scientists around the world. As the NSERC-IBM chair for Women in Science and Engineering, Maria has a five-year plan to double the participation of women in computer science programs. A self-professed game junkie, Maria may have one foot in computer fantasyland, but she's definitely rooted in reality when it comes to making a difference for women in technology.

"If we build it, they will come." This could be Maria Klawe's personal motto, and certainly appears to be the underlying mission behind her lifelong research. If she can help design even one educational game that engages a young mind and stretches her or his imagination, Maria feels that she has done her job. A mathematician at heart, the professor has always done her part to encourage girls to join in her love of numbers. Now she's turned her keen mathematical mind toward the queen of all mathematical machines, the computer. Maria has dedicated most of the last decade to creating interactive games that are inviting to girls and boys. Like Girl Tech founder, Janese Swanson (see p. 208), Maria is certain that the sooner we develop computer games, software, and multimedia with girls' needs in mind, the sooner a new generation of girls will become computer fluent. Sounds like a simple equation, but Maria assures us that this particular problem hasn't been easy to solve.

First, Maria had to put years of research into examining just how boys and girls differ in their approach to and interaction with computers. Most of her cutting-edge Canadian-based research has taken place in the context of E-GEMS—the Electronic Games for Education in Math and Science project—which brings together computer science and education researchers, teachers, and software developers to get to the heart of the computer conundrum. Maria admits that when she started the E-GEMS project back in 1993, she didn't think there was a difference between boys' and girls' computer use. She explains, "It wasn't until we spent two months just watching, watching, and asking, but basically just observing children and trying to find out how they interacted with computers that I finally saw how vast the differences were. I just couldn't believe how different their interactions were."

Maria and her team found that although girls and boys both liked computer and video games a lot, they liked different things about them. Girls cared more about the story line and the main characters. Girls wanted games with positive social interactions, worthwhile goals, and opportunities for creative activities. Boys liked fun, fast action, competition, and violence. Both boys and girls liked adventure, challenge, humor, graphics, sound effects, and music. The research also showed that boys were much more aggressive in getting their "fair share" (or more) of time on the computers and video games. Girls were often reluctant to assert their right to take their turn when it came around, unless there was a researcher there to help them. Finally, convinced that there was indeed a gender gap in computer use, Maria set out to make some changes.

As a mother of two, Maria didn't have to leave home to find out how important computer and video games had become for children. While watching her kids, Janek and Sasha, at play, she first heard the mental click when she realized these games could be used for educational learning as well as entertainment. "They were playing video games, and I became convinced that the best avenue would be to try to . . . put mathematical ideas into the game. So they would be exploring the mathematical ideas, but in a sense doing it as a form of discovery and enjoyment."

Armed with the knowledge that computer games could be a useful model for educational learning, Maria began to experiment. Later, when she realized the huge gap in computer use and fluency between boys and girls, Maria took action to get girls in the game. She asked herself and her colleagues, "Well, what would it take to make computer games that would appeal to girls as well as boys?" As a mathematician, Maria didn't initially see this challenge as falling into her own area of expertise, but eventually she gave up on finding somebody else who was willing to do the research and decided she would put together a team herself.

Never one to shy away from solving an important problem, Maria, in her career track, shows her considerable commitment to research. Since she received her first science undergraduate degree at the University of Alberta in 1973, Maria moved on to receive a graduate degree and then took up various assistant professorship positions across Canada and the United States. In the mid-1980s, she made the move to the corporate world and headed up a mathematics research group at IBM in California. By 1988 she was back at the University of British Columbia, and has since acted in many important academic roles, from head of Computer Science to vice president of Student and Academic Services. She is now the dean of Science at UBC, but the active-minded professor also heads up SWIFT (Supporting Women in Information Technology), a five-year outreach project to encourage girls and women in computer-related careers.

A woman who has been a lifelong student of numbers and patterns, Maria still cites mathematics as her all-time favorite subject. "I've been interested in mathematics education and getting children interested in math my entire life. I did my first TV show on mathematical games for kids when I was 17. If you're a female mathematician, the chances are you've been trying to engage more girls to get more interested in math at some point in your career." A math wiz, an artist, and an amateur musician, Maria defies all stereotypes and cites her pet project, E-GEMS, as a golden opportunity to combine her artistic and mathematical talents. "I live my life visually both when I do my mathematical research and everything else including my art, and E-GEMS has allowed me to combine all my various interests."

Funded primarily by the Natural Sciences and Engineering Research Council of Canada (NSERCC), with support from game publishers and computer companies, including Electronic Arts, IBM, Apple, and HP, E-GEMS has already successfully produced interactive multimedia stories such as Phoenix Quest and Avalanche. Given Maria's proximity to the popular west coast Whistler Mountain Ski Resort, it's not surprising that at least one of her multi-player electronic games is based on the story of an avalanche disaster response team. In Avalanche, the four-person role-playing program asks users to take on the role of either a librarian, scientist, ski patrol warden, or the mayor in a small mountain village setting. Highly interactive and entertaining, the game is designed to address girls' computer preferences for story lines filled with adventure, mystery, and problem-solving. Despite the initial success of both Avalanche and Phoenix Quest, Maria has been frustrated by the same industry challenges as has Girl Tech's Swanson, in her effort to bring these valuable electronic games to market.

Maria's latest multimedia project, Virtual Family, is another innovative effort aimed at giving girls an alternative to the ever-popular "shoot-'em-up games." Girls aged 12 to 14 are encouraged to program their own family-oriented cartoon focused on an entire cast of interactive animated characters. Virtual Family asks girls to jump into the world of JAVA, "rather than take the more traditional and, frankly, often quite boring method of learning how to program." Within an hour-and-a-half of using this unique learning tool, the girls are typing code, and compiling and creating with confidence. So far, the success of Virtual Family validates Maria's findings that girls won't hesitate to embrace the world of computer programming and code if they see the relevance of the task and respond to the story line.

Intimately familiar with the trials and tribulations of trying to bring girls closer to math and science, Maria is probably best fit to respond to those asking, Why bother? Why encourage girls to use computers at all, especially if they show lack of interest? Maria has a quick answer: "Obviously, the way in which we use computers in our everyday life is going to increase. It's going to be absolutely everywhere, and often it won't look like a computer. I think girls will have much richer opportunities and have much to offer if they learn to embrace computers at an early stage." As more women enter the fields of technology design and development, Maria also thinks that we'll see a wider range of creativity in the computer field. "I think that as more women have influence in the marketplace both in terms of buyers, developers, there will be much more of a higher priority put on usability and access."

Maria has spent a lifetime thinking about what is going to help us change, and she's not looking only to other women in the computer industry for answers. Instead, she is putting the challenge to women in the popular media, especially those who are making critical decisions in network television and the mainstream film industry. Maria asks them, "What would we need to do to convince you to work with us on this issue, to get this problem fixed?"

Well, what would it take? The mathematician in Maria is willing to lay odds that we can work together to make a difference.

Anja Haman

Technical Director
Radical Entertainment
www.radical.ca

Everyone measures success in a different way. Some people think they've made it when they're making a lot of money. Others measure their success by counting how many people they have working for them, or how many clients they have. Anja Haman measures her success in, um, a different kind of increment. Cup size!

Anja is the technical director at Radical Entertainment, a software and game-development company based in Vancouver, Canada. She makes video games for a living—but she doesn't like playing them. She's a feminist—but she makes games that would cause a lot of feminists to squirm in their seats. She's a world-class Ultimate Frisbee player—and says that her job has made her better at her sport.

RICK COLLINS

Anja takes pride in her work. She wants to make a difference and to make a positive contribution, but it's hard to fight the evils of the world when you're a video-game developer. Or is it? Turns out that since joining the Radical team, Anja has had many opportunities to make her voice heard and to change the kinds of content and images video-game players pop onto their Sega systems.

The first order of business for Anja when she joined Radical was breast size. Since the industry was new to her, she hadn't realized just how incredibly disproportionate and, well, ridiculous, the female form was being rendered in the video-game market. Once she started to see what was out there, she realized that game developers take gigantic license with body types of female game characters, and that, if left unchecked, that license would only balloon. Literally.

Anja sums it up best herself. "You know, I can't say, 'Let's have an average-sized woman with average-sized breasts that are sort of droopy' . . . I'm not going to get that . . . but what I can do is lightheartedly make fun of the developers for bringing their fantasies to work." Anja tries to get close to reality one bit at a time, and if this year her characters can move from a D cup to a C, maybe next year the video-game divas will be sporting a B.

To Anja, breast reduction is success. If she can get the characters in her games to come a cup size closer to reality, then she's making a difference. But, of course, there's much more to being a technical director than just battling image stereotypes. According to Anja, a technical director is basically a project manager, with a focus on technology issues. She works with producers, art directors, and creative directors. Her job is to find out what the product is supposed to be and then find a technical solution to make the game work. "If you left it up to the programmers, they'd make their own game," Anja says with a chuckle, "so my job is a process of directing them back to the design and marketing requirements."

With a full sense of irony but without a trace of bitterness, Anja recounts a story of one of the first computer science courses she signed up for. She had never used a computer and didn't know what they were for, so, in an attempt to help her understand the concept of computing, the professor chose to use an analogy—knitting. "I'd always been a tomboy. I didn't know how to knit. Nor am I interested in knitting," she laughs. "The professor was going over how knitting is this ordered thing that you can follow, break up a task into little subtasks, you do one row and then can do the other row. He was trying to, I think, make it easier for me to understand what computing science is."

Needless to say, Anja's first introduction to computers didn't go well. She didn't see the point. But she sees the point now, and the incredible enthusiasm and energy that she has for her career make it clear that she's followed the path that's right for her.

"I absolutely adore my job," Anja admits. "It really shocks me how much I enjoy it. I think, to a very large degree, it's the culture that we've set up here. Because you can take risks, you can make mistakes, you can openly admit that you've made an error, and then you can move on.

"And I also work with absolutely wonderful people. They're fun. I can come in here a little bit grumpy because things aren't going well and almost always I'll run into someone who just makes me howl."

It is hard to imagine Anja coming into work grumpy. She's given to uncontrollable bursts of laughter. Besides, Radical seems like an environment that would be hard to be grumpy in—there's no shortage of activity to keep a person chuckling. Extra-curricular activities range from dragon boating and Ultimate Frisbee to soccer, volleyball, and hockey. And during our interview a three-foot-tall Darth Vader—apparently a co-worker's son taking a stroll around the office while his dad is busy writing code—complete with helmet and weapon strolled down the hallway brandishing his weapon. No wonder Anja has fun here.

Anja is living proof of her own belief that new technology companies can be incredible places for women to work. First of all, she says, the high salaries available in this field will help women to gain independence. Salaries are going up because there is a shortage of skilled knowledge workers in her field. Anja knows that these high-paying jobs will continue to be available to women.

But there's more. Anja points out how much variety there is in technology fields and how many different ways there are for women to get involved. She did her BSc in computing science then earned a master's in computer graphics, but she believes that what she does now combines her personality better with her technology background. "Had I not had the technology background, I would never be able to do what I do now. But you don't just have to be a programmer. There are so many excellent jobs out there that are challenging and constantly changing."

The more you learn, according to Anja, the more valuable you are—and she's learning all the time. She believes that video games will truly have "arrived" when they appeal to the mass market because of their narrative, character development and emotional depth. Her work at Radical is motivated by her desire to nudge that dream forward.

She's doing her part to change the world—one project at a time, one game at a time, one changed mind at a time, and, yes, even one *cup size* at a time.

Sandra B. Smith

Senior Program Manager, Virtual Collaboration System
Indaba Communications
www.indaba.net

Sandra Smith is one of the many women working in new media who had never even heard of jobs like hers when she was growing up. Let's face it, guidance counselors, even in the late eighties, weren't always up to date on careers in interactive design, video-game production, or multimedia. And Sandra, like so many others, wasn't encouraged to study computers as a way to pursue her love of the arts. In fact, no two things could have seemed more disparate to her as she graduated from high school and went on to pursue a degree in art history at the University of Delaware.

Happily, though, Sandra is a person who is open to taking risks and pursuing new opportunities when they arise. So even though her career began in the arts, she kept her eyes open and was able to make the leap from arts administration

 to interactive project management to Internet start-up in the blink of an eye. In just a couple of years, she went from waiting tables in Seattle to doing military research with the U.S. Army Rangers for a video game. And she hasn't looked back since.

After school, Sandra traveled to New Mexico and then moved to Seattle in search of an exciting, fulfilling career. In Seattle she worked as a waitress while also doing museum internships, and later landed work in some local art galleries. Sandra then worked for a nonprofit arts organization known as the Center on Contemporary Art (CoCA), where she met a woman who was interested in the coming together of art and technology.

This was something that intrigued Sandra as well. A college friend had received his degree in computer science, and they often spent late nights talking about how their two disciplines would meet someday and produce amazing results. Little did she know that just a few years later she'd find herself combining design, art, and technology to create interactive games for the mass market.

Eager to find a way to explore the juxtaposition of art and technology firsthand, Sandra's colleague at CoCA left to join a small start-up company in Seattle called Zombie Virtual Reality Entertainment; Zombie was developing 3-D video games for the personal computer market. When the position of office manager became available, Sandra decided to join up. She realized this was a great opportunity to get into the interactive industry just when it was starting to grow.

Sandra worked as Zombie's office manager, but quickly demonstrated her creativity and project management skills and was given an opportunity to become an assistant producer on some of Zombie's interactive entertainment products. From assistant producer she was promoted to producer, a role that was perfect for someone able to manage teams, organize large-scale projects, and maintain a creative vision throughout a lengthy production schedule.

The first game Sandra produced was Special Ops. This was the first title in what later became a successful series of games based on the U.S. Army Rangers. Special Ops was one of the earliest interactive shoot-'em-up games to take place in realistic, outdoor, 3-D environments. A player must lead his team of Army Rangers and complete a mission while dealing with counterterrorist attacks, hostage rescues, and reprisal attacks. It is a war game that tries to recreate the action, time pressure, and realism of combat. It was a long way from art school.

Sandra is a strong but soft-spoken woman whose living room is full of art books and antiques, not action adventure posters and war games. She doesn't even own "Risk," and, in fact, war and weapons are the things that most worry her about technology. So when she agreed to take on the incredible responsibility of producing Special Ops, she knew she had her work cut out for her.

Sandra started that work by doing some research. The game's development team consulted with Special Forces military advisors on the design of the missions, and even observed Ranger and Light Infantry Unit "live fires" to get the feel of actual combat. Sandra agreed to try firing a gun as a way to understand the feeling she'd be trying to create for her players (and hated the experience so much she vowed never to pick up a gun again). Instead, she focused on making the game visually rich and realistic. She studied photos of military vehicles, weapons, and equipment, and started to build a production plan for her team.

As the Special Ops producer, Sandra's main responsibilities included drafting design proposals, hiring new employees, creating and managing the production schedules, managing the hefty budget, overseeing the design of the Web site that would promote Special Ops, and writing product documentation. She was constantly faced with decisions about whether a feature should be kept or cut, and was therefore in a position to play a critical role in the outcome of the product. She was also in daily contact with the game's publisher and provided ongoing input into the business development strategies that affected her game. Amid this, Sandra made sure she took a few minutes to play the game every day to see what was working and what the team could do better.

After the successful launch of Special Ops, Sandra found herself in demand. Game companies everywhere were looking for producers, so Sandra decided to take her now proven skill set into a less violent arena. She moved to Massachusetts, where she joined the team at Looking Glass Studios. At Looking Glass, Sandra added another successful title to her resume. She signed on to produce a flight simulation game called Flight Unlimited III. She enjoyed applying her skills to a new game and in a new environment, but found that she missed the west coast. She was also keen to bridge into an Internet career, so when an opportunity arose, she once again decided to take the plunge.

Today Sandra is one of nine employees at a west coast Internet start-up called Indaba Communications. After years of trying, an old college friend successfully wooed Sandra into joining his new company, so she moved back to Seattle and joined the management team as senior program manager of their Virtual Collaboration System. This company is as new as they get, and is sure to give Sandra a chance to galvanize her risk-taking entrepreneurial side.

Sandra and the Indaba team will be working to develop what they hope will be the prime mode of communication for the future. Their technology will allow a group of people to meet in a real-time 3-D environment and share objects and ideas from anywhere in the world. Sandra will work with designers and engineers to create a solution that makes it possible for customers using the system to see and hear each other as if they are in the same room.

Despite the challenges of working in the male-dominated world of video-game and Internet development, Sandra is proud to be a woman in this industry and hopes she's playing a small part in opening doors for other women who might be interested in getting involved. In a world where you are trying to combine the points of view of artists and engineers, and come out the other side with one cohesive product, good managers and communicators play a critical role. In technical or management roles, and in the Web development, learning software, and interactive entertainment fields, Sandra firmly believes, women are as important an asset in the development and growth of technology as they are in all aspects of life.

Bernadette Yvette Lacarte

Computer Graphic Artist, Retro Studios
Austin, Texas
www.retrostudios.com

Bernadette sees art almost everywhere—and creates art everywhere else. Her body is just one of her sketch pads and is full of beautiful images that, like everything about her, illustrate the combination of strength and femininity that make her a courageous example of what women in technology can accomplish.

Bernadette's favorite tattoo is a woman of her own design who lives comfortably on the lower half of her back. As she interprets it, the woman is shedding her skin and becoming the woman she wants to be. What could be more perfect?

With this kind of passion and creativity, it's hard to imagine how Bernadette might have made a living before the emergence of electronic design. It's hard to imagine her

deriving much satisfaction from designing corporate business cards and brochures. Perhaps she would have made documentary films, or painted. But, instead, she became a computer graphic artist.

Bernadette is from Sudbury, a mining town in northern Ontario. She rebelled her way through high school and

JEROME KASHETSKY

bartended her way through university to pay the bills. As an undergraduate she studied fine art, philosophy, and religion. Both before and after school, she did a lot of traveling and exploring. She read for the blind, headed up a summer camp for children, and painted murals for restaurants looking for a splash of color.

Bernadette drew satisfaction from a lot of these things but knew she still hadn't found her calling. She worked at a media-monitoring company and started studying law before deciding it was time to make a move. Like most of us, she wasn't exactly sure what kind of work her arts degree and diverse work experience had prepared her for. She'd always wanted a job that would allow her either to travel to her heart's content or to get paid big bucks to draw pretty pictures. Thanks to computers and the Internet, the latter was about to become a reality.

It was in 1995 that Bernadette's craving coincided with the tumultuous early days of the multimedia revolution. She had always been intrigued by the idea that the Internet was essentially uncharted territory, and saw the digital domain as something just waiting for explorers to uncover it, investigate it, and harness its potential. Bernadette saw her chance to become one of these early Internet explorers when she heard about a new multimedia school opening in Vancouver. Eager to make a move, she left Ottawa, borrowed some money, and went back to school.

Bernadette spent 10 months being introduced to new media in Vancouver, and was captivated. She went from knowing almost nothing about computers to being a top audio, video, and multimedia design student. Her talent was immediately clear to everyone who saw her work, and she knew she had found her calling.

Multimedia design gave Bernadette the opportunity to combine her fine arts training with her management skills and passion for design. Here was a chance to make a living

Don't let the words "it's because I'm a woman" cross your lips. Let the fact that you didn't get promoted challenge you, not discourage you. Let it challenge you to work harder, learn more, or change your environment to one where you will be acknowledged and appreciated.

It's not so much the sexism to watch out for but how you let it affect you. Don't waste your time with other people's hang-ups. Otherwise, this will become another area where women will just have to try their best to "fit in."

as an artist in an environment in which pushing the creative envelope was a requirement.

With her multimedia design certificate in hand, Bernadette was ready to job hunt. Her talent was evident in her portfolio, and her new skill set was in hot demand, so it didn't take long for her to find a job. Shortly after she graduated, a friend told Bernadette about a job designing software interfaces for an electronics company in New York. She emailed some sample designs to the company, had a phone interview, and was hired. That simple.

After a year in New York, Bernadette landed a junior position at a top international videogame company. She'd never imagined herself participating in this industry; in fact, she believed that mass-market video games were essentially sexist endeavors that stereotype women as the buxom warrior, the feeble victim, or the unsightly enemy. The move seemed to be at odds with her strong feminist and philosophical ideals. She discovered, however, that working to develop toys for the mass market is a great way to do things differently. Bernadette was quickly promoted to creative director, where she had a chance to direct the design of the games she worked on and really drive the look and feel of her products.

As a game designer, Bernadette found that she brings something very organic to the visuals of her projects. She also discovered that she brings an important and positive dynamic to her company and her teams. She finds that she entertains different ideas and offers a different outlook on the way a woman fits in . . . both as part of the development team and as a character or game player.

Officially, it is Bernadette's job to be the front-end designer and graphic coordinator for the game she is working on. She creates 3-D interfaces and textures game environments, and also designs all the 2-D artwork for the game (i.e., logos, billboards, cover art). Throughout the long game development process, she is also responsible for ensuring the consistency of the game's visual style.

Unofficially there are other things that Bernadette brings to her work. She brings a woman's perspective to the table in a world dominated by young men. She brings a strong voice to her workplace and believes that if she expresses her opinions clearly enough, someone is bound to hear her. Throughout history, women have effected change in all professions simply by offering a woman's perspective, by enlisting other women, and by voicing the desire to include other women in their research. Bernadette is extending this influence into the world of new-media entertainment. She doesn't deny that there are occasions when she's had to endure sexist comments from a few of the men at work, but it's nothing a quick matronly stare won't curtail, she says.

Today Bernadette is trying her hand at something new—this time in Austin, Texas, where she's joined a company called Retro as its new front-end designer. She'll be coming up with the look and feel for the interfaces of all Retro's new games, a great opportunity to unleash all the creative power she's got stored inside her.

With women like Bernadette climbing through the ranks and revolutionizing the content we load into our computers, the future looks bright. Games are becoming more engaging as interfaces move away from the traditional backdrops of the early shoot 'em ups and car racing games.

Bernadette's desire to bring art to new platforms and her commitment to risk-taking will continue to help her push the limits of computer graphic design. Her talent and unique spirit are reminders that new media creates opportunities for all of us to find spaces that challenge us and roles where we can make a difference.

Jane Siberry
"Melding Music and Multimedia"
www.sheeba.ca

"My record company, SHEEBA, does 85 percent of its mail-order business through the Internet. It would not exist without computers.

When I left Reprise/Warner Bros. in 1996 it was all a surprise. Wha . . .? I said, blinking in the unobstructed light.

Other record companies stepped forward with offers. But after a number of releases on Reprise, I was beginning to feel that a lot of the good energy coming towards me was being wasted simply because the company was too large for someone like myself. A dissipatory effect rather than one of strengthening momentum. And also, after a certain point of Reprise's non-returned investment in me, "critical but non-commercial success," I began to feel a bit like a charity case. I didn't feel I was earning my own keep. I felt the need to reduce and consolidate. On all levels. I had

MIKE TOPF

already started a small [girls' school] fan club a few years earlier. My mother had tended it for a while, advising young girls to stay in school and keep their hair the way that the good Lord intended. Mine was red at the time. I looked at the offers. I looked at my seedling fan club. I stood on the shores of the Internet at the end of the millennium and contemplated my future.

Then the slow galvanizing began. As people started hearing about SHEEBA, it was like watching dots connect. People who had followed me with great difficulty from afar were suddenly able to find me. They wrote tentatively to SHEEBA. SHEEBA wrote back. Confidence grew. People wrote to others about SHEEBA. News was forwarded. Forwardings were forwarded. Forwardings upon forwardings. Exponential. People in small pockets of Siberry-awareness around the world being connected. And with each direct contact made, I felt red lights go up on the map. An energetic grid being silently laid out. A grid of like-mindedness being strengthened.

I pushed off from the shore on the Ship-Called-SHEEBA."

—Jane Siberry, *One Room Schoolhouse,* 1999

From her beginnings in the early 1980s as a guitar- and piano-based folk artist in the coffee houses and clubs of Toronto, through her many musical incarnations, Jane Siberry has redrawn the boundaries of popular music by consistently and courageously taking risks. In 1996, she sailed away from the mainstream music machine on her ship called SHEEBA, and took full control of her career, both creatively and commercially.

As a celebrated musician with a discography that now totals 12 albums, Siberry envisioned her label as a vehicle to pursue projects beyond her recorded work, and to distribute "all things Siberry," including her growing line of books, videos, and merchandise. Jane describes her independent, artist-owned record company as being "fiercely perched on the cliffs, above the shores of the Internet." With an eagle eye, she says, she has watched the shoreline change swiftly in the past few years, and especially swiftly within SHEEBA, making her little company an important schoolroom for herself as an artist, a businessperson, and simply as a person. "Lack of cash has been a great teacher," says Siberry, "but creative control is a rare thing. As head of my own label, I've had a lot of lessons in a short period of time that have put me in a much better position as a human being and a creative person than I was."

One of her first exercises as a student in her self-constructed "one-room schoolhouse" was to design the SHEEBA [www.sheeba.ca] Web site in early 1996. From that point on, the Internet became SHEEBA's infrastructure and Jane's own personal classroom. As a digital student, Siberry took a very organized approach. Working with a designer, she began to translate her unique vision online by creating "the look and flow" of her initial Web site. It took her two months, and Siberry admits it was a huge learning curve, but it was a creative process she enjoyed. All the Web elements—sounds, colors, images, and "triggers"—are carefully chosen by Siberry to reflect her personal esthetic. She says, "My current site happens to all be in white because that's the mood I'm in—bare, stark, and ruthlessly uncluttered."

The musician's wintertime "white site" represents a particular phase of her evolving body of work, but on a deeper level it also symbolizes the Internet as the medium of the new millennium for all artists to explore and expand their art.

In 1998, the "gods" accelerated Siberry into the next level of learning by having her "expand too quickly" in her first two years, which landed her in a crisis. She had to fire two employees, let everyone else go, and take over a huge financial debt. The ship-called-SHEEBA was reduced to a crew of one. But the fledgling business owner moved to a deeper level of understanding of the structure of her own business by learning to program and code her own Web site, navigate accounting programs, and negotiate merchant rates with credit-card companies. Somewhat to her surprise, the mathematical aspects of coding fitted in with the musician's desire for efficiency. "I don't like filler or waste, and so the challenge was to apply my minimalist esthetic to my Web site and my business."

Despite her artistic inclination to dabble in the latest gimmicky software, Siberry was careful not to let SHEEBA become reliant on technology. "It's about the music, not about technology, and I try to keep as much of my system out of the hands of that greedy mistress. It was a terrible feeling when I took over the company in 1998 and couldn't get at things because they were tied up in software programs that I didn't understand. I pulled a lot of things back into a 'hands-on' form. I now have a mix of the two worlds—e.g., fancy accounting software—but I keep a general ledger on paper. I can take it with me to parks and stare at it."

Instead, SHEEBA's mantra became "economy of energy," and Siberry's classical, almost old-fashioned approach influences every aspect of her newly streamlined business. Overall, she asserts that gaining control of all phases of Web site development as well as her entire e-business infrastructure has been particularly "esthetically pleasing and efficient" for her music. She explains: "If someone asked me, 'What do you find sexy?' I'd have to say, 'Mastery.' Whether you're a great musician or a cashier or whatever."

As the "master" of her own digital domain, Siberry has once again proven to be a pioneer.

As a talented musician, Siberry also knows the value of a good instrument. She believes the computer, as an interactive machine, could potentially sharpen our minds and even increase our cognitive abilities. She even heralds the computer as a potential instrument of faith, a digital guide that may inspire us to become more self-aware and perhaps even more spiritual. "The computer teaches people to be more clear about what they want . . . What do people want? What do they pray for? We're not very good at expressing our needs. We don't know how to activate help from the universe. As we 'search for things on the Internet,' we are trained to be clearer in our questions. This act teaches us how to better ask the great computer in the sky for what we want. How to pray."

A belief in the computer's power to connect us convinced Siberry to launch her label. Suddenly left alone without a core of support, she soon realized she didn't have time for her own natural shyness. She conceded that she couldn't afford to be standoffish and that she might have to request help from those outside her own insular musical community. When her Web site first went live in 1996, she had a fictional "Peoria Fontaine," who kept a distance between Siberry and the public. When she took over alone in 1998, she was too busy (and worried) to maintain that arm's-length approach. She took a leap of faith and invited her fans to participate in her work and, to some degree, her life.

Those who found Siberry through the window of her Web site watched her grow and stumble throughout the early years. She readily declares that she sought advice from the public on a variety of topics from "design tips to growing roses," and claims the Internet actually allowed her a forum to "increase rather than decrease the human factor" in her own personal and professional life. An excerpt from Siberry's book, One Room Schoolhouse, encapsulates her belief in the potential of the Internet to connect, enlighten, and empower:

When I send my email newsletter out every month or two, I feel like a spider. A grand dame. In the centre of a web. It is usually late at night when I finish gathering all the news together. I use "spellcheck." Oh. I see "Siberry" must be "replaced." I do a heart and soul check. Alright. I press the SEND button in the wee small hours of the morning and feel the lines move out into the darkness. Across and around the world. Moving towards *the people at the other end of the letter as they are at work or asleep or painting or delivering myrrh and frankincense or in rush-hour traffic on the other side of the world. Words traveling along the great grid like beads of dew. The world wide web. The spider web. Spider. Eight. Infinity. The weaver. Webs upon webs. Angles upon angles. Angels upon angels. The web becomes a sphere, a ball. We look deep into the ball and see ourselves.*

As Siberry began to weave her new Web community, her fans were suddenly startled to receive personal notes from SHEEBA: "Jane . . . is that really you?" The personal touch became an integral part of SHEEBA's new interactive philosophy, whether it involved her response to e-fan-mail or the artist's efficient, but personalized, processing of an order of merchandise. Regardless, the transaction is interactive and the result is that "the eye of the artist is directly in touch with the order."

"With the help of the Internet," Jane says, "I've enjoyed having the mystery removed from the 'artist's life' thing, so that the fans are seeing how it really is!" But Siberry the artist qualifies by adding, "The mystery is removed in order for there to be room for the real mystery. It's not valuable to see artists as just any other human being. There must be recognition of their value as artists; the unique talent or gift that each has to offer. The artist's role is to create a 'larger' world, more elbow room, so to speak, for the time one is within the work. For the person's entertainment, relief, or chagrin. So, in effect we should be careful not to normalize the artist. It is also the artist's job to act as a scout . . . to be the sound of the ocean before the people get there."

Siberry prefers to focus on the value of the Internet as an instrument for achieving greater "synchronicity" between humans. For example, a fan could be listening to one of her songs and then go on the Web and see a poem by Siberry or receive an email from her in response to a query. The possibilities of interaction and authentic relationship are suddenly exponentially increased. Siberry pays tribute to her fans and their newfound level of synchronicity in the foreword of her latest catalogue: "And much of what you see in SHEEBA now is a reflection of this [interaction] and also a reflection of your interested eye. So many spirits coming forward with excellent advice, constructive criticisms. Idealism and realism have done an intimate (and sometimes too public) *pas de deux* in our first three years, but the ship-called-SHEEBA is a sturdier vessel for it."

Jane Siberry's parting words on her SHEEBA catalog act as an invitation to fans and to all of us who may be interested in exploring the uncharted territory of the Internet. She envisions a great flotilla of ships joined together, each of us afloat with our own personal energy, faith, and courage aboard:

All of us on our own ships, triremes, quadremes, cinqueremes. Moving forward on our own personal seas. Heading more often towards the shining parts? More alert to small changes in weather? More knowing when to give the oarsmen a rest? Remembering more often to sleep under the stars? On deck. The shifting, the creaking, the ultimate full sail ahead.

Denise Donlon

Named one of the "25 Most Important People In New Music" by *Shift* magazine in 1998, Denise Donlon may be the most qualified woman in Canada to speak knowledgeably about the intersection of music and technology. Since 1985, audiences have watched Denise develop from on-air host of television magazine, *The New Music*, to host/producer and eventually director of programming at MuchMusic, "the Nation's music station." Throughout her dynamic career, Denise has brought audiences a wide range of reports and profiles on the international music scene and offered a unique perspective on social issues. In her current position as vice president and general manager, MuchMusic, MuchMoreMusic, she is considered to be one of the biggest powerhouses in the Canadian music industry.

As a respected business decision-maker and an avid music fan, Denise has particularly strong opinions about the power of the Internet to revolutionize the music industry. The online delivery of music may, in fact, be one of the biggest changes in music technology in the past century. Like most Internet-inspired innovations, the digital music industry is developing at the speed of light, and Denise is perfectly positioned to explain what the fuss is all about.

With the recent advent of MP3 technology (one method of downloading digital music), Denise has been carefully monitoring the impact of this nascent technology. Touted as a major breakthrough, MP3 has been the subject of much debate in the industry. Denise explains that access to digital music through the Internet allows the average music consumer to have considerably more control over the music. For example, anyone with an Internet connection can download for free, or purchase, any piece of music that is digitally available. This kind of access reaps huge benefits in flexibility and selection, as fans are no longer locked into buying pre-packaged CDs at a local music store, but instead can purchase any of the songs they want and customize their own compilation. Understandably, this new arrangement is potentially threatening to major record companies. Denise sums up the controversy: "On the one hand it is seen as a breakthrough revolutionary artist-friendly format, and on the other side it is seen as the death of the conventional business as we know it."

New and independent artists may also benefit from the emerging digital trend. Via the Internet, the artist could bypass the conventional method of signing with a major record label and instead attempt to promote and sell their own music on the Web. Denise cautions against making this autonomous leap too quickly: "There are many women artists who are trailblazers in these areas, but the problem is that it takes a very special kind of artist to be able to benefit from Internet marketing. Basically, it reminds me of an old 'Who' quote from a *New York Times* article, 'Meet the new Boss, same as the old Boss.' And that is really what it is. Because you can be an artist and you can put your little MP3 logo on your site, and then you can wait while it grows cobwebs for somebody to come and visit you. Ultimately you need to market it. And you need to break through the noise of all of the other Internet sites out there. Breaking through the noise costs money, so ultimately, it is about capital. You will find often that the artists who are successful with this kind of technology are artists who already have a brand name, so they don't have to re-market themselves. These artists would then break or reinvent their ties with their label because

Definition of MP3 technology.

Users of MP3 technology can buy a piece of hardware (usually retails for about $199 US). This equipment is about the size of a Walkman. The user can then go to an MP3 site on the Net and download a song or an album digitally. It is an exact music copy of the music. The music is then recordable and moveable.

the label, of course, owns all of the rights to the artist's music."

Despite the challenges, Denise remains hopeful that the advent of the Internet will help to level the playing field for artists by enabling them to have more control, but she denies that every musician will profit. "I think it is going to take a very certain savvy kind of artist to be able to take control of her own business. Most artists are left-brain creative, sitting in their rooms singing and writing music, and suddenly in order to get caught up in the Internet marketing MP3 world, they would need to muster a competent business side. So, suddenly the artist is consumed with business matters versus artistic matters."

Overall, Denise maintains, the advent of digital technology is really just one of many small revolutions in the history of music. "The bottom line is that the music industry was built on hits. And in the Internet world, the industry is still going to be built on hits . . . hits of a different nature. But the industry will still be consumer-driven."

Nevertheless, she has hope for those who play music on the fringes and especially independent female musicians. "There are major traditional and conservative industry dynamics at play here, and it has only been in the past 8 to 10 years where female artists have risen to the top of the charts in their own right. But there could be a next wave of empowerment for women, because certainly we are seeing a current wave of women in music generally. Now that women have that autonomy, recognition, and a pathway to success, it is a little bit easier than it was, and maybe they will begin to embrace the technology sides of the business as well. I'm sure it will happen."

Recently dubbed Canada's "Queen of Rock," Denise Donlon knows an emerging music trend when she sees it. As one of today's most respected music pioneers, she is perfectly positioned to promote the female talent of tomorrow.

Sara Bailey

Self-Employed Creative Consultant and Multimedia Designer
Turbovision Creative
www.turbovision.com

Artists have long fought internal battles about whether to pursue their passion or to put their creative talent to work in the few arenas that afford solid career options. For people like Sara Bailey, new media has brought an end to this dilemma.

Sara Bailey is artistic. And has always known that she wanted a career that would allow her to pursue her creative talents. She also knew that she didn't want to be a starving, struggling artist, committed to creative freedom but perpetually broke. When Sara graduated from high school she wanted to find a way to be creative while also earning a good living.

With this in mind, Sara set out to explore her options and decided to pursue a career in art therapy. She enrolled

at Toronto's York University in graphic design and psychology, hoping this combination of studies would form a solid foundation for her to begin her career. After a few years, however, she found herself growing tired of both areas of study and decided to take a year off to re-evaluate. In search of inspiration, Sara dropped by the Emily Carr Insti-

JEROME KASHETSKY

tute of Art and Design in Vancouver, where she read about a new program in Electronic Communication Design (ECD). It intrigued her. The three-year program taught graphic design, but also incorporated the basics of traditional and 3-D animation, video editing and post production, and interactive media. The Emily Carr ECD program was the only one Sara applied for that year, and, on the strength of her application and portfolio, she was accepted into a small class of 14 students.

Sara quickly excelled at school, and in her third year of studies at Emily Carr she received a tuition scholarship. One of her instructors, Deborah Shackleton, saw her presentation and asked Sara if she wanted a job in the summer, designing a prototype for a CD-ROM educational project Shackleton was working on. The project, to develop a professional practices resource for artists and designers, turned out to be one of the most influential experiences in Sara's career.

The job took Sara, along with fellow student Corina Rothlisberger, traveling around Canada and the U.S., interviewing and videotaping prominent artists and designers. It was a dream come true. Sara and Rothlisberger interviewed 20 artists in five cities in less than two weeks. They met interesting, successful creative people, including the creative director of INStyle magazine and the director of programming at Bravo!

ICQ is an instant messaging program that enables you to connect directly with friends, family, and colleagues when you are both online. Send an instantaneous message and get a quick reply (a faster alternative to email), send and receive files and URLs, or start up a person-to-person (or multi-person) chat. ICQ has many other add-on features but the best part is seeing that friends are online and saying "Hi!"

Judy Renouf
Content Strategist
Blast Radius
www.blastradius.com

Even before Sara's career had started, she was able to find out how other creative people had built successful businesses and careers, and she was able to take that knowledge with her as she began her own job search.

As it turned out, Sara's talent and tenacity made her job search less difficult than she'd imagined. She landed a job with The WebPool Syndicate, an Internet start-up whose creative director knew he wanted to hire her the minute he saw her work. She jumped on board and became an integral part of the creative vision that would define the WebPool over the next few years. She was learning new skills every day and building an impressive portfolio that became her ticket to success.

Since her early days with the WebPool, Sara has brought her Web design talent to companies including television stations and educational software developers. No matter what the focus of her work, she always works hard to understand her audience, maintain design integrity, and work with her clients to create products they can be proud of. Eventually, her work became so sought after that she decided to become a freelancer so she could choose which projects to work on rather than being tied to a single company.

Today Sara works with clients including Cossette Communications, the Canadian Broadcasting Corporation, and Douglas Coupland. Her days are filled with everything from scheduling and billing, to educating her clients about technology and the production process. She is constantly running off to meetings with contacts, clients, and potential clients, and has an endless stream of design deadlines to keep her occupied. Sara is also committed to keeping herself educated about the latest technologies and solutions so that she is always able to provide her clients with up-to-date information.

Being a freelance creative consultant definitely gives Sara

the flexibility she wants, but it's a lot of work. On a typical day Sara wakes up early and spends the morning getting graphics files ready for the clients she'll be meeting that day. She rushes off to client meetings or to wherever she's going to be consulting that day, constantly working with teams to plan Web sites or evaluate new designs for a project. When she gets home, Sara quickly checks her email, fires off responses to the most urgent messages, and then usually logs on to ICQ to catch up with friends and colleagues with whom she's working. After dinner, she actually does most of her designing. She'll sit in front of her computer with her cat and work on new screen designs she's been dreaming up. When she's at the beginning of a project, she uses this evening time to look for inspiration in books and other design materials she's collected. Her boyfriend, Sang, has his computer across from hers in their home office, so while she's working, Sang keeps her amused by surfing the Web for weird sites or video clips to inspire her.

Already a successful creative consultant, Sara's not sure what's next for her. What she does know is that the new-media environment is the perfect playground to experiment in while she figures that out. Looking back at the days when traditional designers had to spend hours doing paste-ups and drawing is enough to convince her that she would never have had the patience to be a designer before computers came into popular use. "Of course, the computer is just another tool and cannot replace the creative process," she acknowledges. "But it sure can speed it up."

Char Davies

Virtual Artist
www.immersence.com

Char Davies wants to literally immerse you in her art. As a traditionally trained artist, she now experiments with cutting-edge computer technologies to explore already familiar subjects: nature, the body, time, and space. Building on these themes, she then creates interactive virtual environments and invites you to fully participate within these artfully constructed spaces.

A visit to Char's self-designed Web site [**www.immersence.com**] is the first plunge into appreciating her unique art form. The simple but effective site acts as a virtual gateway to understanding her intricate three-dimensional explorations of nature and also archives her growing body of work.

For almost 20 years, Char has been slowly interweaving her painting techniques, first with film and later with 3-D

computer graphics and animation. As an artist, she was beginning to feel frustrated by the two-dimensional picture frame and began to seek ways to go beyond it. Fueled by her desire to communicate her ideas, her search finally led her to experiment with computer technology. She also reveals that her move from painting to a new art esthetic was in part caused by her own near-sightedness. "I turned my attention as a painter to investigating my own extremely myopic eyesight. In doing so, I was initiated into an alternative experience of space whereby "objects had apparently disappeared; where all semblance of solidity, surface, edges, and distinctions between things . . . had dissolved." Consequently, Char abandoned the medium of painting for that of 3-D computer graphics—a medium that offered "the possibility of creating in virtual three-dimensional on the other side of the picture plane."

In 1988, Char became the founding director of Montreal-based start-up computer graphic software company Softimage. Taking a slight detour from her art, she and her team focused on business-building and developing state-of-the-art technological tools. Soon, Softimage software became known worldwide as a tool to achieve the epitome of the kind of realism that can be attained with computers. It was even used to animate all of the dinosaurs in the blockbuster film Jurassic Park. Computers were revolutionizing the film industry, and suddenly visual artists were creating an entirely new animated artform.

In her own art, however, Char was much more interested in moving as far away as possible from reality. She began to dabble with her company's innovative software and soon discovered that the same technological tool that could bring dinosaurs back to life on the big screen could also take her art to a new level of expression within VR or what Char prefers to call "immersive virtual space."

Since 1994, Char has created two virtual environments, Osmose and Ephemere, drawing on the natural world for her inspiration. To enter these works, you wear a head-mounted display that enables you to see 3-D computer graphics and hear sounds generated in real time by an SGI supercomputer. Char maintains that every person's journey is different—"What you experience depends on your behavior and location within the work. Your breath and balance are tracked by an interface vest. Breathing in causes you to rise; exhaling causes you slowly to fall. Leaning gently lets you change direction."

Both works reveal Char's unique and personalized version of nature. For 15 minutes, users can travel through forests, move through running water, or delve down through the earth. Images are soft, semitransparent, and luminous; the entire virtual experience is deliberately designed to move away from any common concepts of reality. "I was deliberately seeking to develop an alternative to what most VR was at the time, which was again, hard-edged, based on a kind of an attempt at realism."

Many of the more than 10,000 people who have been immersed in these two installations reported the experience had triggered a heightened response. Char claims that she didn't intend to evoke certain emotions in people, or certain experiences. "I wanted to create this alternative, more contemplative, receptive mode. So it surprised me, the first time the work showed publicly, that many people were quite emotionally overcome by it—unprepared, surprised—and would have all these emotional experiences that ranged from euphoria to people crying afterwards, out of a kind of sadness and a nostalgia and a sense of loss that they couldn't even put into words."

Char's choice to design these evocative landscapes stemmed from a desire "to light a lamp in a dark corner," a phrase she uses to demonstrate to other people that virtual reality is capable of something far more mysterious, and rich, than "shoot-'em-up" games. "I didn't want to do 'shoot-'em-up' games, and this is where, maybe, a more female sensibility comes into play. I wanted to create spaces where it wasn't about 'doing.' It was not about running around and doing things, and scoring, and having an adrenaline rush based on speed. I was more interested in creating what I have named 'a slow rush.' My environments might foster contemplation, receptivity, heightened perception, and create a situation in which the participant might let go of their desire to run around, you know, really fast and speedy, and instead let go and just be in the space."

Char is also cognizant of the importance of her virtual work in a "real" world where we are increasingly losing our ability and perhaps our desire to protect and cherish nature. To some, her immersive installations act as a warning that one day virtual environments might be all we have left. Those who enter her animated, 3-D models are potently reminded of how extraordinary it is to be fully conscious of our natural living world.

Jill Scott

Video and Performance Artist

Australian video and performance artist Jill Scott uses her art to explore the relationship between the body, history, and technology. Her installations and experimental exhibitions have appeared in galleries throughout the world and reflect Jill's own philosophies, politics, and personality.

One of her most recent works, "Frontiers of Utopia," is a computerized sound and video installation that interactively presents the lives of eight 20th-century women. As users, we are invited into the experiences, opinions, and memories of these characters, who are linked by their attendance at a Virtual Dinner Party. Through a series of multimedia techniques including archival footage, sounds, and graphics, the user can click their way through each woman's autobiography and even initiate dialogue between any two characters at the dinner table. As participants in the computer scene, we are invited to delve into the development of

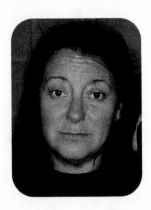

these virtual characters over time as they evolve their various perspectives and politics based on events that happen to them and around them.

In a recent interview, Jill, 47, says that "Frontiers" is actually the last of three works about memory, idealism, and technology. "Before this, in fact as early as 1976, I created interactive performance artworks which fed these issues, including the use of video surveillance in installations. I was always interested in the idea that the viewers could become performers in the installation space or editors of various parts of information about the relationship between history and herstory, idealism, and the body."

Some of the characters in "Frontiers" reflect Jill's personal experiences. For example, one of the characters, Gillian, is based on Jill's own student-radical Marxist days in Melbourne in 1968. "When people meet this character, they remember their own idealism and they say they still believe in basic levels of class equality and education. But now, upon reflection, they can better identify certain levels of propaganda and conformity. 'Frontiers' is popular in Europe because the eight different levels of idealism represented are still in discussion."

Jill also uses her art to frame her own views on topics ranging from feminism to body politics. "Frankly, these are my views and I am not ashamed that they show how old I am. Firstly, I still believe that women are 50 percent of the world's population and in this light they must be given a voice—by both women and men. This of course included the old feminist ideas of equal pay and equal representation. Now, I am interested in a type of resistance from within the system rather than an escape, and I think that if women do not get involved in technology they will be left out of it in the future. If they ignore the implications and ethics of genetic and microbiological processes on their bodies, they may well be left out of the future altogether."

Note: Some quotes are adapted from previous interviews with international journalists Katy Deepwell and Josephine Greis.

Kathy Hammer

Womenshands.com
www.womenshands.com

Kathy Hammer wanted to get rid of the middleman and see if she could connect female artisans with the people who most appreciated their world. The result: Womenshands.com. The Web site is a global community where message boards and chat-rooms capture exchanges on everything from traditional quilting to titanium furniture design.

The woman behind the Web site is Kathy Hammer. Twenty-five years after she and Oxygen Media founder Gerry Laybourne (see p. 79) became friends, the duo debated this question over lunch: "How do you link female artisans with their customers?" During a chat at Oxygen's New York headquarters, Kathy says her original idea was to figure out how to use new media and new technology to link artistically inspired women from all over the world. "Creative women, businesswomen, or artists, whatever. I wanted to see how we could use technology to eliminate the kind of middle roles, the middle stuff that happens so many times between what women, particularly creative women and artisans, make . . . and where their products ultimately get sold."

The idea of using television and converged media came from Gerry. "I had the sort of formula, and Gerry felt really strongly that, besides making the work available, besides letting people know about the work, we should tell the stories of women behind the work—both on television and on the Internet. She was completely right: women respond to stories, they respond to relationships. And you know, it's a very, very powerful idea."

Just three weeks after the site's launch, the feedback from women was overwhelming. "What's happened in, really, just a little bit of time since we launched is [that] hundreds and hundreds and hundreds of women have been sending ideas about what they do, that is creative, in their lives." Kathy seems astounded at what she's created, and even more surprised at the impact technology had as a tool to create the global community connection.

Who are the female artisans Kathy, personally, was excited to connect with via her Womenshands site? "One is a black woman in Buford, North Carolina, an indigo textile artist who's traveled to Africa to learn about indigo-dying and weaving of textiles. And the other woman, sort of at the other end of the spectrum, lives in Oklahoma. I love this woman. I truly love her idea: she makes these sort of stick-figure paintings of women and she does it with three dimensions, in glitter-gold spray paint! Totally wonderful."

Kathy hopes her Web site will inspire others to express their own creativity, perhaps start their own businesses, and explore their own cultures. As the site evolves, so do new ideas for the future.

Sharon Hyman

Autodocumentary Filmmaker
Machartis Productions
www.mlink.net/~sharon

Sharon Hyman is building a career at the intersection of film and technology. The filmmaker has worked in film and community television for more than a decade and has witnessed firsthand how the movement evolved as a tool for social change.

As a former Educational Technology master's student, Sharon, 38, specialized in the design of film and television programs to promote social learning and attitude change. In turn, it seemed natural for her to combine her interests as an educational technologist, activist, and community television producer to promote social change. In fact, Sharon says, the community television movement in Canada began as a means of providing an alternative voice for disenfranchised people. Today, Sharon is excited about new tech-

nologies and their emerging potential as a new medium for giving the average citizen a global voice and a forum to tell their own stories.

Since her teenage years, Sharon has been exploring the autodocumentary genre. As a young woman, she felt that this style—namely, turning the camera back upon oneself to tell one's own stories—offered her the freedom to present a perspective of the female experience not typically seen in the mainstream media. She had discovered the power of film to challenge the status quo, and felt compelled to create original works that were funny, yet highly provocative.

Sharon's exploration of the autodocumentary continued throughout her academic career, as she discovered the versatility of the video camera. The advances in small-format film and video have allowed her to experiment further with autodocumentary. Most film productions involve piles of people, yet her last film, *Arousal*, was shot without a crew. Some scenes were even shot alone, just Sharon and a tripod. And Sharon is the one on screen!

While pursuing her undergrad and grad studies, she continued to experiment with autodocumentary. As a teen, she had worked primarily with Super-8 film technology, but as a grad student, she began enjoying the emerging video-camera technologies. "So I have been afforded great freedoms, in terms of controlling all aspects of the production, from writing the scripts to the final editing process. In turn, I am allowed to present my own vision on screen, which is a rare and wonderful thing for a visual artist. Especially since my perspective is a feminist one, and has always been since my teenage years."

Sharon feels that the evolution of film and video technologies has also helped female artists gain entry into the male-dominated film and television industries, and will continue to do so with the new line of digital video cameras, which can produce broadcast-quality images for a fraction of the cost they used to incur. "I think women still face the additional stresses of having to constantly 'prove themselves' (especially if they are members of a minority group). The other day I was asking a fellow filmmaker about video cameras, and he just naturally assumed that I was a researcher, not a director."

Sharon believes anyone who challenges the status quo will have a hard time, and she believes this is especially true for women. "It is always a risk to challenge the dominant voices of society, and women and/or members of minority groups typically already have less power in society, and thus stand to lose more. I think there's still a 'male culture' in the IT world, and in the film world, and this puts additional stresses on women. Male counterparts often have a sense of entitlement to their power, while women seem to have to earn it over and over again."

In an effort to use technology to help her take control of her own career, Sharon also designed a promotional Web site called Machartis Productions. "The site has made conducting publicity so much easier. I am really excited by the potential of the Internet to promote independent film, as exemplified by the phenomenal job done by the *Blair Witch Project* people. It's wonderful how the Net is democratizing the distribution game, allowing independent producers to compete with the major studios, who have million-dollar publicity budgets. My films hopefully demonstrate to people that a good film can be made without big crews or budgets, as long as there is real passion and commitment behind the project."

Sharon is continually reinventing her "one-woman" film productions: finding new ways to produce/write/star in her own films, using no crews and very simple equipment setups.

Check out one of her films . . . coming to a URL near you.

URL Glossary

AAUW (American Association of University Women)
www.aauw.org

APC Women's Networking Support Program
www.gn.apc.org/apcwomen

Apple
www.apple.com

Blast Radius
www.blastradius.com

Blue Zone Entertainment Inc.
www.bluezone.net

Bravo! Canada
www.bravo.ca

Breakup Girl
www.breakupgirl.com

The Bulldog Group
www.bulldog.com

CBC (Canadian Broadcasting Corporation)
www.cbc.ca

Canoe
www.canoe.ca

Cebra Inc.
www.cebra.com

City Interactive
www.cityinteractive.com

Coolgirls
www.coolgirls.net

Coolwomen
www.coolwomen.org

Credo Interactive Inc.
www.charactermotion.com

CTVNews.com
www.ctvnews.com

eBay
www.ebay.com

Ecmarket
www.ecmarket.com

EDventure
www.edventure.com

EFF (Electronic Frontier Foundation)
www.eff.org

E-GEMS (Electronic Games for Education in Math and Science)
www.cs.ubc.ca/nest/egems/home.html

Electronic Arts
www.ea.com

Ellie Rubin
www.ellierubin.com

Emigre Fonts
www.emigre.com

Excite
www.excite.com

Extend Media
www.extendmedia.com

Fast Company
www.fastcompany.com

Girl Tech Inc.
www.girltech.com

Great Canadian Story Engine
www.storyengine.ca

Harvard
www.harvard.edu

Hewlett-Packard
www.hp.com

IBM
www.ibm.com

ICANN (Internet Corporation for Assigned Names and Numbers)
www.icann.org

ICQ
www.icq.com

IICS (International Interactive Communications Society)
www.iics.org

Immersence
www.immersence.com

Indaba Communications, Inc.
www.indaba.net

Intel Corporation
www.intel.com

Inventive Women
www.inventivewomen.com

ITAC (Information Technology Association of Canada)
www.itac.ca

iVillage
www.ivillage.com

IWT (Institute for Women and Technology)
www.iwt.org

Journeywoman
www.journeywoman.com

Jparker Company
www.jparker.com

Lotus Development Corporation
www.lotus.com

Lucent Canada
www.lucent.ca

Lucent Technologies
www.lucent.com

Lycos
www.lycos.com

Mainframe Entertainment Inc.
www.mainframe.ca

Marimba, Inc.
www.marimba.com

The Markle Foundation
www.markle.org

MIT (Massachusetts Institute of Technology)
www.mit.edu

MIT Media Lab
www.media.mit.edu

Mitsubishi Electric Corporation
www.mitsubishi.com

Moxie
www.moxie.ca

MP3.com
www.mp3.com

MSNBC
www.msnbc.com

MuchMusic
www.muchmusic.com

Neurofunk
www.neurofunk.com

New Profit Inc.
www.newprofit.com

The NRG Group
www.thenrggroup.com

NSERC (Natural Sciences and Engineering Research Council of Canada)
www.nserc.ca

Nua
www.nua.ie

Oprah Goes Online
www.oprahgoesonline.oxygen.com
www.oprah.com

Oxygen
www.oxygen.com

Pseudo Online Network
www.pseudo.com

Quicken Canada
www.quicken.ca

Radical Entertainment
www.radical.ca

Retro Studios
www.retrostudios.com

SeniorNet
www.seniornet.org

SHEEBA Records
www.sheeba.ca

Shenetworks
www.shenetworks.com

Shift
www.shift.com

SoftImage
www.softimage.com

Sony
www.sony.com

Speakers' Spotlight
www.speakers.ca

Spirit Ware Fashion Design
http://spiritwarecanada.com

Spotlife
www.spotlife.com

Sun Microsystems
www.sun.com

Switch-On.co.uk
www.switch-on.co.uk

TecKnowledge
www.tecknowledge.com

Turbovision Creative
www.turbovision.com

Vancouver Television
www.vancouvertelevision.com

WebCrawler
www.webcrawler.com

Webgrrls International
www.webgrrls.com

Webmonkey
www.webmonkey.com

Webnoize
www.webnoize.com

Whatis
www.whatis.com

Wired Woman Society
www.wiredwoman.com

Women Action 2000
www.womenaction.org

Womenshands.com
www.womenshands.com

Women'space
www.womenspace.ca

Xerox Parc
www.parc.xerox.com

Yahoo!
www.yahoo.com

Yahoo! Canada
www.yahoo.ca

ZDTV
www.zdtv.com

Zero-Knowledge Systems Inc.
www.zeroknowledge.com

Zombie Virtual Reality Studios
www.zombie.com

Acknowledgments

The list of people we wish to thank is long. From the first days of our planning, to the final editing of the book, we have felt enormously supported by our families, colleagues, and friends.

Our immense gratitude to our editor, Don Loney, for his immediate recognition of this book's value and for championing it through the publishing process with warmth, wisdom, and calm determination. And to the entire Harper-Collins team particularly, Roy Nicol, Karen Hanson, Doré Potter and Charlotte Shiu, who each brought their own ideas, generosity, and patience to *Technology With Curves*. Thank you as well to Allyson Latta for doing such a complete and thorough copyedit.

There are a number of people we especially want to thank for the part they played as we brought our ideas into book form: Victoria Ridout, Sarah Crawford, Denise Donlon, Carol Stephenson, and Don Tapscott. Thanks as well to Jerome Kashetsky, a wonderful photographer, for his generous donation of time and talent, and for the wonderful images he captured for *Technology With Curves*. A special thank you to Sara Bailey for sharing her design expertise (as well as her story) with us. Her work on our book cover helped us capture the essence of *Technology With Curves*, and her contribution of talent to the creation of www.technologywithcurves.com makes us look good online as well. And to Christina Rodmell for being as passionate about *Technology With Curves* as we are and helping us to spread the word about our book with her usual grace and expertise.

And finally, we want to thank the women who shared their stories with us for their willingness to open up to strangers and offer their insights, opinions, and experiences. They have educated and enriched us.

—The authors, 2000

from Denise . . .

To Emma and JoAnn whose email addresses I know as well as my own. Thanks to both of you for embarking on this expedition in virtual storytelling.

I also want to thank some of my special friends and colleagues who made contributions to this book in myriad heartfelt ways: Ingrid Bron, Joyce Barnes, Pino DiMascio, Deborah Fulsang, Stephen Haberer, Christopher Kelly, Denise Lawson, Shari Swan, my entire Wired Woman Toronto leadership team, and research assistant Michelle Poirier. My particular gratitude to Kelly O'Neill and Moe Poirier for their creative coaching, advice, and imagination.

Thanks as well to Toshiba of Canada, Palm Canada, Xerox Canada, Bell Canada, Fujitsu Canada and IBM Canada, for providing me with the tools necessary for keeping pace with technology.

And finally a sincere thank-you to all of my friends and family for their encouragement and support, especially to my beloved parents, Sharon and Bill, my sisters Sharlane and Crystal, and my brother, Dean.

from Emma . . .

To Denise and JoAnn, two brave and creative women who made the writing of Technology With Curves an adventure in virtual communication and a pleasure throughout.

Heaps of gratitude to Barry, my husband, who is always the first to believe that my ideas are good ones and who supported me through each and every *Technology With Curves* tumult. Thanks as well to my parents, Christine and Roger, and my sisters, Sarah and Hannah, who I know will be as proud of *Technology With Curves* as we will.

For me *Technology With Curves* has always been a testament to the women who inspired this book and have inspired me throughout the history of Wired Woman and my own technology career. Anja, Wired Woman's first ever guest speaker, continues to remind me that our efforts in technology are valuable but also sometimes comical. I am grateful to her and all of our *Technology With Curves* women for their willingness to share their trials and triumphs with us.

And lastly, from among the many friends and colleagues who have supported me over the past few years, I want to single out Alissa Antle, Shannon Emmerson, Chris Gilmour-Lammerse, Kathryn Grafton, Farrah Jinha, Cary Low, Judy Renouf, Deirdre Rogers, Mike Howatson and Jenny Winterbottom for their enthusiasm about *Technology With Curves* and their contributions to making it a reality.

from *JoAnn* . . .

To Denise and Emma, much thanks and gratitude for this editorial adventure.

The wisdom and guidance of some great people, primarily Agnes Kell-Napier, David Napier, and James Warner, helped shape this book. Thank you, sincerely.

And my gratitude goes as well to Matt and Jan Napier for their support, and Dr. Luke Napier, for his friendship and for the Manhattan digs as an interim editorial base.

Many people contributed to this book, but I would like to send very special thanks to Shelby Betancourt and Andrea Pernstich, Elissa Barnard, John LeBlanc, Peter Gnemmi, Andrew Bowins, Denis De Klerck, Jeanine Smartt, Eric Mason, Dr. Dan Reid, Robert Godhue, Betsy Judelson, Ann-Marie MacDonald, David Morelli, and Mary Wiens.

Finally, to Paul Baran, Dr. Anita Borg, and my late father, Dr. Robert Warren Napier. Thank you for inspiring me by your words, your work, and your enduring examples of lives well lived and stories well told.